Oriental Step-by-Step Cookbook

General editor: Miriam Ferrari

International Culinary Society
New York

Note:
All recipes serve 4.

General editor: Miriam Ferrari

Copyright © 1990 Arnoldo Mondadori Editore S.p.A., Milan
English translation copyright © 1990 Arnoldo Mondadori Editore S.p.A., Milan

Translated by Elizabeth Stevenson

This 1990 edition published by
International Culinary Society
distributed by Outlet Book Company, Inc., a Random House Company, 225 Park
Avenue South, New York, New York 10003

ISBN 0-517-035693

8 7 6 5 4 3 2 1

Typeset in Great Britain by Tradespools Ltd, Frome, Somerset
Printed and bound in Italy

Contents

Introduction

Oriental cooking is today enjoying great popularity. This can partly be explained by the wealth of Chinese, Japanese, Thai, Vietnamese, and Indian restaurants in Western cities where one can try out new and exotic dishes and also by the increasing number of people who visit these countries and wish to recapture the flavor of the Orient in their own homes.

The recipes chosen for this book are among the most well-known and important dishes in traditional Oriental cuisine. Each recipe has been adapted slightly, according to the availability of certain ingredients in Western shops. They are set out in clear and easy stages, the more elaborate dishes being illustrated with step-by-step photographs so that the more complicated procedures are easy to follow.

The introductory chapter contains basic techniques and recipes and the book also includes a comprehensive glossary listing typical ingredients and utensils. These invaluable sources of reference ensure that a successful meal can be conjured up with ease.

Oriental cuisine is an art in itself. It can only fully be appreciated by taking part in the preparation and cooking of the food as well as by eating it. This book aims to help you recreate this art.

Basic preparations and techniques

Opposite: the ingredients for garam masala.

Below: clarified butter (ghee). Bottom: Japanese basic stock (Niban dashi, second stock).

Basic stock (Japan)
Ichiban dashi (first stock). Place 1 piece *kombu* (seaweed) in a deep pot and fill with 4$^1/_2$ cups water. Bring just to boiling point, then remove the seaweed, drain, and reserve it. Add 1 cup bonito flakes and 1 tbsp light soy sauce to the boiling water, stir and remove from the heat. Strain the liquid, reserving the bonito flakes.
Niban dashi (second stock). Prepare in the same way as *Ichiban dashi* above, reusing the seaweed and the flaked bonito. The first stock is for soup, the second for use in main dishes and sauces.

Chicken broth (China)
Makes 6–8 cups. Place the carcass and any other bones of 1 chicken in a deep pot full of boiling water. After 1 minute drain and transfer the carcass and bones to a pot containing 12 cups/5$^1/_4$ pints fresh boiling water flavored with 2 tsp grated root ginger, 1 chicken broth cube, and 1 tbsp saké (rice wine). Continue to boil until the liquid is reduced by about half. Strain before use.

Instant Japanese stock
Basic Japanese stock (*see* above) can be made from a freeze-dried product, *dashi no moto*, by simply dissolving the contents of the packet in water. Although convenient, this product inevitably does not taste as good as freshly made stock.

Clarified butter (*ghee*)
Melt unsalted butter very slowly in a heavy-based saucepan until the butter is translucent and the whitish residue has settled on the bottom. Skim off the surface scum and pour the clear fat through cheesecloth into a clean bowl. Clarified butter is very useful; it can withstand very high cooking temperatures without burning and will keep in the refrigerator for up to 4–5 months.

Mandarin pancakes (China)
Serves 12. Blend 2 cups all-purpose flour and $^1/_4$ cup boiling water. Gradually add sufficient cold water to mix to a smooth dough. Knead for 5 minutes, cover with a cloth and leave to stand for 20 minutes. Using your hands, roll the dough into a long sausage and cut it evenly into 24 pieces. Roll these out into very thin disks and brush one side of each with sesame seed oil. Sandwich 2 pancakes together, oiled sides inward, and fry in a wok oiled and heated to a very high temperature until bubbling. Cool slightly, then separate the pancakes and fold in half, oiled side inward.

Chinese boiled rice (Pai fan).

Wonton wrappers (China)
Mix 2 parts all-purpose flour with 1 part water, add a pinch of salt, and beat to a loose, elastic consistency. Leave to stand for 1 hour. Wipe a heavy skillet with an oiled cloth. Using your finger, smear a circular film of batter 6 in in diameter onto the warmed griddle. When a paper-thin pancake has formed, remove it very carefully with a spatula so as not to break it. Repeat until all the batter is used up, wiping the griddle frequently with the greased cloth.

Garam masala (India)
Here is one of several home recipes for this versatile mixture of spices. Mix together 6 tsp black peppercorns, 5 tsp coriander seeds, 1 tsp cumin seeds, and 1½ tsp cardamom seeds. Bake for 10 minutes in a preheated oven (425°F). Leave to cool then pound to a fine powder. *Garam masala* is always added toward the end of the cooking time.

Panir (India)
Bring 11 cups/4⅓ pints milk to a boil, lower the heat, and simmer for 30 minutes. Remove from the heat and add 2 tbsp lemon juice and a pinch

of salt. Leave to stand for 10 minutes. Pour into a large strainer lined with cheesecloth and leave to strain overnight.

Boiled rice
The preparation of boiled rice in Oriental cookery varies from country to country.
Pai fan (China). Rinse 2¼ cups rice. Place in a saucepan with 2 cups water, bring to a boil and simmer slowly, partially covered, for 12 minutes. Turn off the heat and leave to stand, fully covered, for 5–10 minutes.
Gohan (Japan). Wash 1 cup short-grain rice, rubbing the grains between your fingers. Leave to drain for 30 minutes. Put the rice in a saucepan with 1½ cups pint water. Bring to the boil, stir and partially cover. Simmer for about 15 minutes without stirring again. Remove from the heat. Leave to stand for 10 minutes fully covered.
Chawal (India). Rinse and drain 1 cup basmati rice thoroughly. Place in 2¼ cups boiling salted water acidulated with a few drops of lemon juice. Simmer uncovered for 13 minutes. Remove from the heat, and stir in 1¼ tbsp ghee.

Curry sauce (*kari*) (India).
Peel and chop 2 cloves garlic and 1 small onion. Heat ½ cup ghee in a casserole and sauté the garlic and onion. Add 1 tsp ground coriander, 1 tsp turmeric, and 1 tsp cayenne pepper followed by the main ingredient of the dish (meat, fish or vegetable) already prepared for cooking according to the directions of the recipe. Stir-fry for at least 5 minutes. Add sufficient water to cover then simmer until tender. Just before serving, add 1 tsp *garam masala*.

In the West "curry" is a borrowed term widely used to describe certain commercial blends of ground spices. They have little resemblance to real Indian curry which derives its distinctive flavor from individually cooked fresh spices rather than a blended powdered form.

Sesame sauce (*goma zu*)
To make this sauce simply liquidize the following ingredients in a blender: ½ cup sesame seeds, 3 tbsp *niban dashi* stock (see above), 2 tbsp light soy sauce, 1 tbsp saké or dry sherry, 1¼ tbsp white wine vinegar, ½ tsp monosodium glutamate, ½ tsp sugar, and salt to taste.

Peanut sauce (*sans katjang*)
Chop ½ onion and fry in a saucepan with 2 tbsp peanut oil. When soft, stir in 1 chopped clove garlic

Panir, fresh curd cheese (India).

and 1 chopped chili pepper; sauté for 2 minutes, then add 1¼ tbsp light soy sauce, ½ tsp cane sugar, ½ tsp salt, 1 tbsp lemon juice, and 1 tsp shrimp paste. Finally, add 2 tbsp coconut milk and 1 cup peanut butter, blend thoroughly, and cook until the sauce thickens.

Chili sauce (*sambal ulek*)
Chop 12 red chili peppers and 1 clove garlic and fry in oil until soft. Add salt to taste. Remove from the heat, allow to cool then put through a blender.

Dough sheets for *hsao mai* (China)
Combine 2 cups all-purpose flour and a pinch of salt with the boiling water. Mix thoroughly, cover with a cloth, and leave to stand for 30 minutes. Knead for 3 minutes. Shape the dough into a

sausage, cut it into 36 equal portions, and roll each piece into a circle about $2^3/_4$ in in diameter.

Sharbat
Bring $2^1/_4$ cups water to a boil, add $2^1/_4$ cups granulated sugar and stir until it dissolves. Add 1 small stick cinnamon, 10 cloves and 10 green cardamom seeds. Simmer until a thick syrup forms. Add $^1/_2$ tbsp rose water and food coloring of your choice. Stir.

Cooking methods
There are more than 40 different cooking methods in Oriental cuisine. The following three are the most common:

Steaming. A bamboo steamer produces the most authentic results. Arrange the ingredients in a single layer in the steamer over a saucepan of boiling water. Fish, meat, and dumplings should be cooked over high heat, eggs, and tofu (bean curd) over low heat. Bamboo steamers can be stacked to enable you to cook a whole meal simultaneously.

Deep-frying. For best results cook in 2 or 3 stages and constantly check the oil temperature. In the 2-stage method, fry until the food is two-thirds cooked. Remove the food, drain, and then resume frying at a higher temperature. In the 3-stage method, cook until the batter begins to set. Bring the oil to the original temperature and fry until the food is two-thirds done and beginning to brown. Complete the cooking process in the final stage by increasing the oil temperature.

Stir-frying. Cover the bottom of a wok with a good layer of oil and heat to a high temperature. Draw off the oil and replace only the amount of oil needed in the recipe. Add the ingredients to the wok one after the other (liquid ingredients are usually added last), stir-frying quickly and continuously at a high temperature. When two-thirds done, transfer the food immediately to a serving dish. It will finish cooking in its own heat.

Tea
The proper requisites for tea-making, according to the Chinese ritual, are fresh water boiled once only preferably in an earthenware kettle and a teapot and cups in porcelain or chinaware.

Thandai (India)
Grind 10 green cardamom seeds, 1 tbsp blanched almonds, 1 tbsp shelled pistachios and a pinch of saffron in a blender. Place the mixture in a bowl with 6 tbsp milk; mix thoroughly, add 6 tbsp sugar, $^1/_4$ tsp turmeric and $^1/_4$ tsp ground nutmeg. Stir well, and serve with crushed ice. In some regions it is enhanced with spirits for special occasions like the Feast of Spring and the Feast of Light.

Roasting spices
Most spices can be dry-roasted before use. It helps to preserve their aroma if cooked just 2–3 minutes over very low heat in a nonstick saucepan, turning continually to prevent them from scorching. Sesame seeds should be closely watched and removed from the heat before they start leaping in the saucepan. For some purposes roasting is done directly over the heat. The spices are then either used whole or ground and mixed together, depending on the recipe method, which often involves stir-frying in *ghee* or oil. Preparations like *garam masala* (see above) partially lose their aroma if cooked for more than a few seconds and therefore should be added to the saucepan just before serving.

China

The Chinese philosophy of life, based on the search for a perfect state of balance, is also reflected in Chinese attitudes to food. A first course could become a main course accompaniment, and a single dish the basis of a whole meal. What is important is to follow one's instinctive sense of harmony in the interplay of flavors, colors and textures.

Climate and environment account for the regional peculiarities of Chinese food. To the north, in the province of Shantung, birthplace of Confucius, and the province of Hopei, where Peking is, the climate is too cold to grow rice. Along the plains of the Yellow River, however, corn, millet, barley, and other cereal crops provide an abundance of flour types which are the basis of many delicacies such as the paper-thin pancakes that are traditionally served with Peking Duck.

To the south, rice reigns as a supreme staple, together with an impressive variety of fish and crustacea, for which culinary experts of old would compete in inventing the most flavorsome sauces. Fried food comes in many forms such as the traditional Cantonese spring rolls. Steamed dishes also abound.

To the more temperate east, there is a large variety of vegetable produce, meat, and fish. Rice and noodles with vegetables enriched with sauces are the favorite dishes for staving off the sharp winters of Shanghai. Here the soy sauce is exceptional and the dry pickling and fermented products are equally excellent.

To the west we find the ubiquitous use of spices, which were introduced to China by Buddhist monks. In these parts the chili pepper, eaten fresh or in powdered form, dominates the cooking scene.

Shrimp toasts

Preparation: 1 hour

¹/₄ cup fresh pork fat ● 4 oz white fish ● 4 quail's eggs ● ¹/₂ cup shrimp ● 2 tbsp water flavored with leek and ginger ● 1 egg white ● 1 tbsp saké or dry sherry ● salt and pepper ● pinch monosodium glutamate (optional) ● 2 tbsp cornstarch ● 8 slices white pan loaf ● ¹/₂ cup white sesame seeds ● ¹/₄ cup flaked almonds ● 1 small thin slice ham ● parsley ● oil for frying

1. Cut the pork fat and the white fish into thin strips. Chop the strips into dice. Boil the quail's eggs, shell, and set aside.

2. Peel the shrimp and remove the black vein. Pound all the ingredients except for the quail's eggs together with a knife.

3. Place the mixture in a bowl and add the flavored water, followed by the egg white and the saké. Add a pinch of salt and pepper and the monosodium glutamate, if used.

4. Stir vigorously until the mixture is smooth. Mix in the cornstarch.

5. Arrange 4 slices of bread in 2 pairs and remove the crusts. Cut each pair into 4, and cut off the corners of the quarters to make 8 small rounds.

6. Roll half the mixture into small balls 1 inch in diameter. Lay 1 ball between 2 rounds. Gently press the slices together smoothing the sides with a knife to prevent the mixture from squeezing out. Coat the sides with sesame seeds.

7. Cut the remaining slices of bread into 8 oval shapes. Cover half of the ovals with a little of the mixture and press a quail's egg into the filling. Cover this with the ham and a little parsley. Spread the rest of the mixture on the remaining ovals. Stick the almond flakes into the mixture vertically to create a pine cone effect.

8. Heat plenty of oil to a temperature of 250°F. Deep-fry the shrimp and sesame toasts, gradually increasing the heat to 350°F.

Five-color hsao mai

Preparation: 30 minutes

1 tbsp peanut oil • 2–3 egg yolks • 12 oz onions • ¹/₂ cup cornstarch • 1¹/₄ cups ground pork • 20 dough sheets for *hsao mai* (see p.11) • seaweed to taste • 3 slices ham • 3 dried Chinese mushrooms, soaked and drained • 1 small can crabmeat

For the seasoning: 2 tbsp saké or dry sherry • ¹/₂ tsp salt • ¹/₂ tsp sugar • 1 tbsp soy sauce • pinch monosodium glutamate (optional) • 1 tbsp sesame seed oil • pepper • pinch ground ginger

1. Prepare the scrambled egg for the topping: heat the peanut oil in a wok, add the beaten yolks, and break up gently with a fork as they set.

2. Prepare the filling: finely chop the onions and using your fingers, blend in the cornstarch.

3. Mix together the ingredients for the seasoning. Put the minced pork in a separate bowl, add the seasoning, and stir to a sticky consistency.

4. Add the floured onion and mix everything together using your hands.

5. Shape a round hole with your thumb and forefinger. Lay a dough sheet over the hole to form a little bag, put a drop of filling in the center, and push it down, supporting the dumpling bag with your hand.

6. When you have filled all the dough sheets in this way, decorate them with a selection of toppings: chopped seaweed, ham, Chinese mushroom, scrambled egg, and crabmeat.

7. Grease the bottom of a bamboo steamer with oil. Arrange the dough cups in a single layer, cover, and place in a wok or saucepan containing boiling water. Steam over high heat for 9–12 minutes.

Spring rolls

Preparation: 30 minutes

2 tbsp cornstarch • $^1/_2$ cup lean pork or chicken cut into 2-cm/$^3/_4$-in strips • 2 tbsp peanut oil • $^1/_2$ cup bamboo shoots, chopped into $^3/_4$-in slivers • 2 dried Chinese mushrooms, soaked, drained and finely sliced • 1 small leek or onion, chopped • 12 wonton wrappers (see page 9)

• 1 tbsp all-purpose flour • oil for frying
For the sauce: 1 tbsp sugar • pinch salt • $^1/_2$ tsp monosodium glutamate (optional) • $^1/_2$ tbsp dark soy sauce • 2 tsp light soy sauce • 2 tbsp chicken broth (see p.9) • 1 tbsp peanut oil • 2–3 drops sesame oil

1. Mix the cornstarch with the meat. Leave to stand for a few minutes.

2. Heat the peanut oil in a wok. Stir-fry the meat, the bamboo shoots, and the mushrooms for 1 minute.

3. Add the ingredients for the sauce. Stir-fry until the liquid has evaporated. Add the leek. Transfer everything to a plate and leave to cool.

4. Prepare the sealing agent for the wrappers: mix 1 tbsp each all-purpose flour and cold water. Add 2–3 tbsp boiling water and stir.

5. Place a strip of filling on to each wrapper. Lift one side of the wrapper, fold over the filling, tuck in the edges, and roll up neatly to form a smooth parcel, sealing the final flap with the sealing agent.

6. Heat plenty of oil in a wok and deep-fry the spring rolls at 360°F. Serve crispy and hot.

Steamed pork and rice balls

Preparation: 50 minutes

²/₃ cup glutinous (pudding) rice • 2 cups ground pork •
1 egg white • 3 tbsp soy sauce • 2 tsp sugar • 1 tbsp saké or
dry sherry • peanut oil

1. Rinse the rice and leave to soak overnight in fresh water. Drain thoroughly.

2. Place the ground pork in a bowl. Add the egg white, soy sauce, sugar, and saké. Using your hands, work the ingredients into a smooth paste.

3. Grease your hands with oil. Shape the mixture into 1-in balls by squeezing a small handful through thumb and forefinger.

4. Spread the drained rice onto a plate. Roll the balls in the rice, pressing lightly to ensure they are all evenly coated.

5. Using a pastry brush, smear the bottom of a bamboo steamer with peanut oil.

6. Arrange the rice balls in the steamer leaving a little space between each ball. Place the steamer in a wok with boiling water. Cover and cook over moderate heat for 30 minutes.

Sweet and sour beef balls

Preparation: 1 hour

1½ cups ground beef • ½ egg • ½ tbsp salt • 2 tbsp cornstarch • 1½ tbsp water • oil for frying • 1 onion • 4 green peppers • 4 slices pineapple • 1 chili pepper • 1 clove garlic
For the sweet and sour sauce: ¼ cup broth • 4½ tbsp sugar • 1 tbsp soy sauce • 2 tbsp wine vinegar • 1 tbsp saké or dry sherry • salt

1. Chop the ground beef, if necessary, to ensure it is perfectly smooth. Place in a bowl and blend with the egg, salt, half the cornstarch, and the water.

2. Roll the mixture into small, even-sized balls 1-in in diameter.

3. Heat plenty of oil in a wok to 350°F. Fry the meat balls until golden brown, turning them gently with a wooden spoon. Remove and drain.

4. Peel the onion and cut into fine slices. Halve the sweet peppers vertically and remove the seeds; drain the pineapple and chop both into small pieces.

5. Remove the seeds of the chili pepper and cut it into ¼-in rings. Set aside. Chop the peeled clove of garlic. Mix the sauce ingredients in a separate bowl.

6. Heat 1½ tbsp oil in a wok. Sauté the garlic; as soon as its aroma is released, add the chopped pepper, onion, and pineapple.

7. Stir-fry the pepper, onion, and pineapple. Add the meat balls and stir-fry, then add the chili rings. Pour in the sweet and sour sauce; mix together quickly.

8. When the sauce begins to bubble, thicken it by adding the remaining cornstarch mixed with a little water. Stir thoroughly.

Beef and Chinese white radish in soy sauce

1 lb trimmed lean beef • 1 tbsp saké or dry sherry • 5–7 tbsp soy sauce • 1 tbsp cornstarch • oil for frying • 1 leek (white part only) • 4–5 fine slivers root ginger • 1 star anise • 2¼ lb Chinese white radish

Preparation: 3 hours

1. Cut the beef into 1-in cubes, place in a bowl, and sprinkle with the saké and 2 tbsp soy sauce. Add the cornstarch. Mix with your hands.

2. Heat 2 tbsp oil in a wok. Stir-fry the beef cubes over high heat until golden brown. (Shallow-fry if you wish the beef to be a deeper brown.)

3. Remove the meat and drain, reserving the juices. Place the meat in a heavy saucepan. Slice the leek into diagonal rings, and chop the ginger. Add these to the saucepan and pour in 6–7 cups water.

4. Add the star anise and 2 tbsp soy sauce. Bring quickly to a boil, skim the surface, cover, and simmer over reduced heat for about 2 hours.

5. During the cooking check the seasoning and add the soy juices if necessary.

6. Peel and cut the white radish into 1½-in pieces. Cut the pieces in half or if very large, in vertical quarters, smoothing the ends with a knife.

7. When the meat is nearly done add the white radish pieces and continue to simmer slowly.

8. Test again for seasoning when the liquid has reduced by half. If necessary add the remaining soy sauce and continue simmering until the white radish is very soft.

Chicken with cashew nuts Szechwan style

Preparation: 20 minutes

8 oz chicken breast • $^1/_2$ egg white • 1 tsp cornstarch • pinch salt • oil for frying • 3 green peppers • 4 oz canned or parboiled bamboo shoots • $^1/_3$ cup cashew nuts • 1 tsp chopped garlic • 1 tbsp saké or dry sherry • pinch monosodium glutamate (optional)
For the sauce: 1 tbsp black bean paste • 1 tbsp soy sauce • 2 tsp sugar • $^1/_2$ tbsp wine vinegar • $^1/_4$ tsp salt

1. Cut the chicken breasts into $^1/_2$-in cubes. Coat with egg white, sprinkle with the cornstarch, and add a pinch of salt.

2. Stir-fry the chicken in a little oil at 200°F until fork-tender. Set aside.

3. Halve the peppers, remove the seeds and pith, and chop into $^1/_2$-in squares.

4. Cut the bamboo shoots into $^1/_2$-in cubes. Mix the sauce ingredients in a bowl and set aside.

5. Stir-fry the cashew nuts in a skillet with a little oil over moderate heat until crisp and golden.

6. Heat 2 tbsp oil in a wok. Fry the garlic until its aroma is released, add the bamboo shoots and the diced peppers, and stir-fry for 1–2 minutes.

7. Add the chicken and cashews. Sprinkle on the saké, pour on the sauce, and stir-fry for a little longer adding the monosodium glutamate at the last minute, if used.

Szechwan chicken with chestnuts

Preparation: 1 hour 30 minutes + 24 hours soaking time

15 dried chestnuts • 3 boned chicken thighs • 1 leek • 1 small piece root ginger • 1$^1/_2$ tbsp soy sauce • 1 tsp saké or dry sherry • pinch salt • pinch pepper • cornstarch • oil for frying • 1 cup chicken broth

1. Soak the dried chestnuts in water for 24 hours. Boil until tender.

2. Cut the chicken thighs into largish chunks.

3. Thinly slice the leek and ginger.

4. Place the chicken, leek, and ginger in a bowl. Add the soy sauce, saké, salt, and pepper. Mix together and leave to marinate for 30 minutes to allow the flavors to soak into the meat.

5. Lift out the chicken pieces, drain, and reserve the marinade. Wipe the chicken clean of any clinging condiments using kitchen towels. Coat the pieces with cornstarch. Heat some oil in a skillet and brown the chicken until crisp and golden. Remove.

6. Pour the broth into a casserole. Add the marinade and the chicken pieces. Bring quickly to a boil, reduce the heat to a simmer, and cook for 20–30 minutes.

7. Remove the leek and the ginger with a slotted spoon. Add the well-drained chestnuts and continue cooking until they have absorbed the juices (about 10 minutes).

Paper-wrapped
Cantonese chicken

Preparation: 1 hour

5 oz boned chicken breasts • 3 Chinese dried mushrooms •
1 small piece root ginger • 1 small bunch chives • 2 oz
canned or parboiled bamboo shoots • 2 tbsp frozen peas •
12 heat-resistant cellophane leaves or waxed paper, 6 × 6in
• peanut oil
For the marinade: 1 tsp soy sauce • ¹/₂ tsp salt • 1 tbsp saké
or dry sherry • pinch pepper • 3–4 drops sesame oil •
pinch monosodium glutamate (optional) • 1 tsp cornstarch

1. Remove the white sinew from the center of the chicken breast.

2. Slice the chicken breast into bite-sized pieces. Soak the mushrooms in water until they plump up.

3. Drain the mushrooms, remove the tough stalks, and cut the caps in thin slices. Peel the ginger and cut into small strips.

4. Cut the bamboo shoots in strips and chop the chives. Pour boiling water over the peas.

5. Place the chicken pieces in a bowl together with all the prepared vegetables. Add the marinade ingredients and mix well with chopsticks.

6. Spread the cellophane or waxed paper squares on a board. Brush the middle of the squares with oil. Place one twelfth of the chicken and vegetable mixture on the greased center of each square.

7. Join diagonal corners of the square to form an upright triangle. Fold the top end of the triangle downward; fold the sides inward then tuck in the corners at the base of the triangle.

8. Gently heat the peanut oil and fry the cellophane or paper cases, turning often until the meat is golden brown. Unwrap at table.

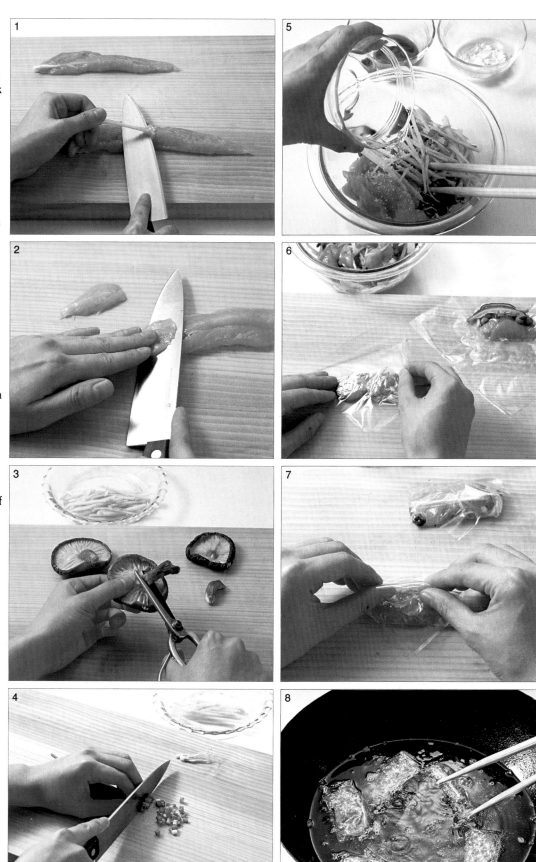

Sweet and sour pork

Preparation: 25 minutes

³/₄ lb pork tenderloin • 1 chili pepper • 2 leeks • ¹/₂ small can pineapple chunks • 4 green peppers • 1 egg • 2 tbsp cornstarch • oil for frying • 1 clove garlic • 1 tbsp saké or dry sherry
For the sauce: ¹/₄ cup wine vinegar • 1 tbsp soy sauce • 4¹/₂ tbsp sugar • 1 tbsp tomato ketchup • 2 tbsp Worcestershire sauce • ¹/₂ tsp salt

1. Cut the pork in slices ¹/₂ in thick. Pound lightly on both sides with the blunt edge of a knife or a meat mallet to tenderize, then cut into bite-sized portions.

2. Remove the seeds of the chili pepper. Cut the pepper into small rings. Cut the leeks into 1-in slices.

3. Drain the pineapple chunks and chop. Halve the peppers, remove the seeds and pith, and cut into portions the same size as the pork.

4. Mix all the ingredients for the sweet and sour sauce thoroughly.

5. Dip the pork pieces in the beaten egg. Roll the pieces in half of the cornstarch then fry in 2 tbsp oil over moderate heat until cooked through.

6. Sauté the garlic in a wok with 1¹/₂ tbsp oil. When the aroma begins to be released, add the leeks followed by the green peppers.

7. Stir-fry until the leeks and peppers are almost cooked. Add the chili, the pineapple pieces, and the meat, stir-frying continuously. Flavor with the saké.

8. Pour in the sauce, stirring quickly. Dilute 2 tsp cornstarch with 4 tsp water. Add to the sauce to thicken. Mix thoroughly and turn off the heat. Serve with boiled rice.

Pork belly with bamboo shoots

Preparation: 1 hour 30 minutes

1¼ lb pork belly in one piece • 14 oz canned bamboo shoots • 2 tbsp oil • 1 small piece root ginger, finely sliced • 4 tbsp soy sauce • 2 tbsp sugar • 1 tbsp saké or dry sherry

1. Cut the pork belly into 1-in cubes.

2. Cut the bamboo shoots crosswise into pieces the same size as the pork belly.

3. Heat the oil in a wok. Fry the ginger slices, add the pork belly, turn up the heat, and stir-fry until the meat is an even golden brown.

4. Transfer the pork belly to a heavy-based saucepan or casserole. Add the bamboo shoots, the soy sauce, sugar, and saké. Pour in just enough water to cover the ingredients. Stir well.

5. Bring to a boil. As soon as it boils, turn down the heat and simmer very slowly for about 1 hour. Allow the liquid to reduce to almost nothing before serving.

Peking duck

Preparation: 5 hours 30 minutes

1 duck weighing 6¹/₂ lb • 2 tbsp molasses • 12 scallions or leeks • 24 Mandarin pancakes 10 cm/4 in in diameter (see p.9)
For the sauce: 4 tbsp sugar • 4 tbsp sweet soy paste • ¹/₂ cup water • 2 tbsp sesame seed oil

1. Wash the duck and cut off the feet if not already done.

2. Make a small incision in the neck under the head. Remove the windpipe and gullet. Insert a straw deep down between the skin and the flesh. Blow air between the skin and the flesh.

3. Slit the belly at the vent end and draw out the entrails and internal organs.

4. Rinse the inside of the duck; wash all over with cold water, drain, dry thoroughly, and sew up the cavities.

5. Remove the wing tips. Tie the duck firmly by the neck and hang over a bowl.

6. Pour $4^{1}/_{2}$ cups boiling water over the duck. Leave for a little to dry. Dilute the molasses in 1 cup boiling water; pour all over the duck. Leave the duck in a dry place, if possible in the sun, for about 4 hours until the skin has completely dried. Lay the duck, breast down, in a large roasting pan. Cook in a preheated oven at 400°F for 20 minutes. Turn and roast the underside for a further 20 minutes. Remove from the oven, stand the roasting pan in another, larger, pan containing boiling water and simmer for 5 minutes over low heat before returning it to the oven and roasting the duck again for 20 minutes on each side.

7. Make as many 1-in slits as possible around the ends of the scallions or leeks. Plunge in iced water and leave until the cuts fan out into "brushes."

8. Remove the duck from the oven. Carve into small slices. Make the sauce: amalgamate the sugar, the soy paste, and the water. Heat the sesame oil in a wok, add the sauce mixture, and stir-fry until it thickens. Each person takes a Mandarin pancake, dips the scallion, or leek into the sauce, brushes the pancake, and lays duck and scallion or leek pieces on top. The pancake is then rolled up and eaten with the fingers.

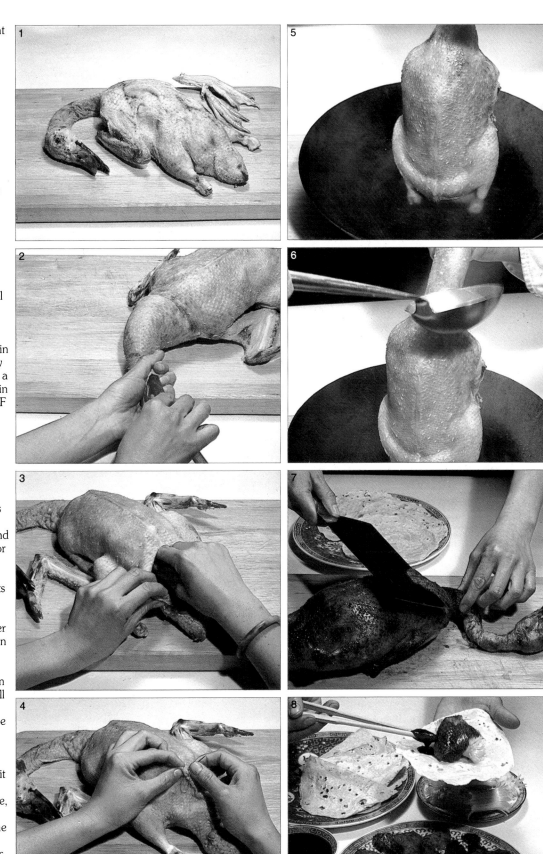

Cantonese fried cuttlefish

Preparation: 25 minutes

2 large cuttlefish ● 1 tsp ginger juice (see below) ● 1 tsp saké ● 2 tsp cornstarch ● 1 medium-sized onion ● 4 large fresh Chinese mushrooms ● 3 oz cooked bamboo shoots ● 1 4-in carrot ● 2 oz snow peas ● 2 tbsp shortening
For the sauce: 1 tbsp saké ● 1 tbsp sugar ● 1 tsp salt ● ¹/₂ glass water

1. Place the cuttlefish in a bowl containing plenty of cold water. Pull off and reserve the tentacles. Gently press the tail end, pull out the head, and discard the ink sac and central bone. Cut open and skin the cuttlefish; remove the fins. Cut the flesh diagonally, then into 1-in pieces.

2. Extract the ginger juice by squeezing a small piece of root ginger through a garlic press. Sprinkle the ginger juice and the saké over the cuttlefish. Allow the condiment to absorb, then sprinkle on 1 tsp cornstarch. Boil the cuttlefish for a second. Drain.

3. Slice the onion vertically into 8 parts. Chop the onion. Discard the mushroom stalks and quarter the caps. Cut the bamboo shoots into rectangles.

4. Cut the carrot into flower-shaped ¹/₄-in slices. Simmer for a minute. Trim the snow peas and cut in half. Simmer for another minute in boiling salted water to bring out the color.

5. Mix the sauce ingredients together.

6. Melt the shortening in a heated wok. Stir-fry the vegetables starting with the onion then, in order, the mushrooms, the bamboo shoots, the carrot. Pour on the sauce.

7. Add the cuttlefish. Mix thoroughly and add 1 tsp cornstarch diluted with water to thicken. Add the snow peas, and serve.

Deep-fried crab claws

Preparation: 40 minutes

12 crab claws • 6 oz shrimp • 2 tbsp pork fat • 1 egg • $^2/_3$ tsp salt • 2 tsp ginger juice (*see below*) • 1 tbsp saké or dry sherry • all-purpose flour • 50 g/2 oz breadcrumbs • 2 cups oil for frying • 1 small bunch parsley • 1 lemon • pepper (optional) • tomato ketchup (optional)

1. Remove the crabmeat from the claws. Finely chop the flesh and reserve the claws.

2. Wash and peel the shrimp, remove the central black vein with a cocktail stick and chop the flesh with a knife.

3. Chop the pork fat, mix with the shrimp, and continue chopping until both are finely minced. Place in a bowl.

4. Separate the egg. Add the white to the shrimp mixture, add the salt and ginger juice (obtained by crushing pieces of peeled root ginger in a garlic press to extract the juice), and mix thoroughly. Add the crabmeat, mix again, then divide the mixture into 12 balls.

5. Stick the base of the claws in the crabmeat balls leaving the pincers exposed. Dust the crabmeat with flour.

6. Mix the egg yolk with 1 tbsp water. Coat the balls first with egg yolk then with the breadcrumbs.

7. Heat the oil to 350°F. Deep-fry the balls until golden brown.

8. Place the parsley in the center of a serving dish. Distribute the 12 crab balls in a circle with the pincers pointing inward, resting on the parsley. Garnish with lemon wedges and season if wished with pepper or tomato ketchup.

Butterfly shrimp with spicy sauce

Preparation: 25 minutes

16 uncooked jumbo shrimp (saltwater crayfish) • 1 tsp chopped garlic • 1 tsp chopped ginger • 1 tbsp chopped leek • 1 tbsp saké • 1 tsp cornstarch • oil for frying
For the sauce: $^1/_2$ cup chicken broth • $^1/_2$ cup tomato ketchup • 1 tsp salt • $^1/_2$ tsp sugar • 1 tsp tabasco sauce

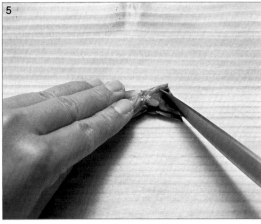

1. Wash and drain the shrimp. Loosen and remove the head by bending the joints inwards and downward. Remove the shell, but leave the tail on.

2. Using a knife, slit the back down to the penultimate joint at the tail end; spreadeagle the shrimp. Do not cut too far or the flesh will part.

3. Remove the black nerve with a cocktail stick.

4. Rinse and dry the shrimp on kitchen towels. Cut off the tips of the tail with scissors.

5. Spread out the opened shrimp on a board. Squeeze out any remaining moisture by pressing the tail joint with a knife.

6. Heat 6 tbsp oil in a wok to 350°F. Carefully immerse the shrimp holding them by the tail; fry for 3 minutes, turning with chopsticks; remove and drain.

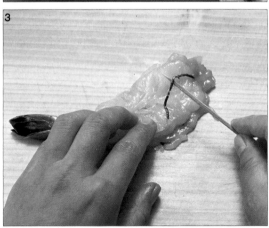

7. Clean the wok. Heat 2 tbsp fresh oil. Sauté the garlic, leek, and ginger for 1 minute. Add the shrimp.

8. Pour in the saké and the sauce ingredients; stir well, so the shrimp can thoroughly absorb the flavors, then thicken the liquid with the cornstarch diluted in 1 tsp water. Cook for a moment longer and serve.

Tea eggs

Preparation: 1 hour

6 eggs • 2 tsp tea leaves • 1 star anise • 1 tsp sugar • 1$^{1}/_{2}$ tsp soy sauce • 2$^{1}/_{2}$ cups water • 2 small cucumbers • 1 tsp hot fermented soy paste • 1 tsp salt • few drops sesame oil

1. Hard-boil the eggs.

2. Roll the eggs against a surface, pressing gently so as to form tiny cracks in the shell, without rupturing the thin inner skin. Do not remove the shells at this stage.

3. Place the eggs in a saucepan with the tea, the star anise, the sugar, half the soy sauce, and the water. Cook over moderate heat for 1 hour, turning the eggs now and then so that they color evenly.

4. When the eggs are stained a deep brown, take out of the saucepan and leave to cool in the liquid. Gently remove the shells, taking care not to pull away the delicate membrane under the shell.

5. Halve the cucumbers lengthwise. Score the skin in a trellis pattern, then cut into small sections. Place in a bowl and sprinkle with the salt. When the cucumber pieces soften, sprinkle with a little water and drain. Mix the fermented soy paste with the remaining soy sauce and the sesame oil. Add the cucumber pieces and stir.

6. Arrange the cucumber pieces in the bottom of a serving bowl or dish and lay the tea eggs on top.

Scrambled eggs with shrimp

Preparation: 30 minutes

5 oz uncooked shrimp • $^1/_2$ egg white • 1 tsp cornstarch •
3 tbsp oil • 6 eggs • $^1/_2$ tsp salt • $^1/_2$ tsp sugar • pinch
monosodium glutamate (optional) • 3–4 tbsp peanut oil •
2–3 tbsp saké or dry sherry

1. Peel the shrimp.
Remove the central black
nerve with a cocktail stick,
wash, and drain.

2. Place the shrimp in a
bowl with the egg white
and the cornstarch. Mix
well, using your hands.

3. Warm the oil in a wok
to 230°F. Add the shrimp
and stir carefully. When
they change color, remove
immediately with a slotted
spoon and drain.

4. Whisk the eggs. Add
the salt, sugar, and
monosodium glutamate (if
used). Mix together.

5. Empty the wok then
heat the peanut oil in it.
Pour in the egg mixture
and stir-fry with a spatula
until half cooked.

6. Add the shrimp and
mix quickly. Sprinkle on
the saké while the eggs are
still soft, stir briefly, and
transfer to a serving dish.
Serve hot.

Five-color omelet

Preparation: 20 minutes

2 slices cooked ham • ¹/₂ bunch scallions • 3¹/₂ oz boiled fresh or canned bamboo shoots • 3 fresh Chinese mushrooms • 6 eggs • ¹/₂ tsp salt • ¹/₂ tsp sugar • pinch monosodium glutamate (optional) • 2–3 tbsp oil

1. Cut the ham into thin strips. Chop the scallion tops into 2-in lengths, discarding the white bulbs. (Chives may substitute the scallion tops, if preferred.)

2. If fresh bamboo shoots are used, wash with care then cut into strips the same size as the ham. Discard the mushroom stalks and cut the caps into similar strips.

3. Beat the eggs in a bowl.

4. Add the salt, the sugar, and the monosodium glutamate (if used). Mix briefly.

5. Add the prepared vegetables to the egg mixture and beat slowly for a few seconds.

6. Heat the oil in a wok. Pour in the egg and vegetable mixture and cook until just set, using a spatula to distribute the ingredients evenly in the wok.

7. When the omelet has set on top, divide into 2 or 3 portions and turn over. Scoop the portions together again.

8. Cook the omelet until it is a nicely rounded shape again. Cover, lower the heat, and leave for a minute or two before serving.

Fried eggplants in sesame sauce

Preparation: 25 minutes

1 tbsp white sesame seeds • 1 chili pepper • 1 clove garlic • 1 tbsp vinegar • 1 tbsp sesame seed oil • 2 tbsp soy sauce • 1 tbsp sugar • 6 eggplants • oil for frying

1. Roast the sesame seeds briefly on a baking tray or under a hot broiler.

2. Remove the seeds of the chili pepper. Cut the pepper into thin rings.

3. Mince the garlic.

4. Place the vinegar, sesame seed oil, soy sauce, sugar, sesame seeds, chili pepper, and the garlic in a bowl and mix well.

5. Trim and wash the eggplants; cut in half lengthways. Score the skin diagonally and deeply without cutting right through.

6. Heat plenty of oil to 325°F in a wok, add the eggplant halves, and fry, turning occasionally, until tender. Remove and drain on kitchen towels.

7. Arrange the eggplants on a serving dish. Pour the sauce evenly over the eggplant and allow it to become absorbed before serving.

Stir-fried beans with mushrooms

Preparation: 20 minutes

9 oz green beans • 1 cup button mushrooms • oil for frying • 1 tsp salt • 1 cup water • 2 tbsp soy sauce • 1 tsp sugar • 1 tsp saké or dry sherry • pinch monosodium glutamate (optional) • few drops sesame oil • 1 tsp cornstarch (optional)

1. Trim, wash, and dry the beans. Cut into 2-in lengths.

2. Wash the mushrooms, wipe dry, and cut the larger ones in half.

3. Heat the wok and when hot add sufficient oil to cover the bottom.

4. When the oil begins to smoke, add the beans; stir-fry, coating them thoroughly with the oil.

5. Allow the beans to absorb the oil then add the salt and the water and cover. Simmer until the beans are tender. Transfer the beans to a plate; empty the wok of liquid.

6. Reheat the wok; pour in 2 tbsp oil. When it sizzles, add the beans and stir-fry, together with the mushrooms.

7. Mix the soy sauce, sugar, saké, and monosodium glutamate (if used) and pour into the wok. Sprinkle on a little sesame seed oil.

8. If the sauce is too liquid, mix the cornstarch with a little water and stir in. Cook for a minute longer. Serve.

Fried rice with smoked salmon and chicken

Preparation: 20 minutes + 2 hours standing time

$3\frac{1}{2}$–5 oz smoked salmon • $\frac{1}{3}$ cup oil • $3\frac{1}{2}$ oz boneless chicken breast • 2 eggs • pinch salt • pinch monosodium glutamate (optional) • 3–4 Chinese leaves, shredded • 1 tbsp chopped leek • $1\frac{3}{4}$ lb cooked long-grain rice • pinch pepper
For the seasoning: $\frac{1}{4}$ tsp salt • pinch monosodium glutamate (optional) • pinch pepper • 1 tsp saké or dry sherry • $\frac{1}{2}$ tsp cornstarch

1. Cut the smoked salmon into strips and set aside.

2. Cut the chicken into slivers. Mix the ingredients for the seasoning and sprinkle over the chicken. Leave to stand for 2 hours.

3. Beat the eggs and season with salt and monosodium glutamate (if used).

4. Heat 1 tbsp oil in a wok. Add the eggs and mix gently until scrambled into small pieces. Transfer the scrambled egg to a plate. Heat $1\frac{1}{2}$ tbsp oil in the wok, stir-fry the chicken until tender, remove, and set aside.

5. Clean the wok and pour in the remaining oil; lightly stir-fry the leek, add the cooked rice, amalgamate the two then add the smoked salmon and the chicken. Stir-fry everything for 3 minutes. Taste for seasoning, add the pepper and, if necessary, more salt and monosodium glutamate (if used).

6. Add the egg and Chinese leaves, cook for $\frac{1}{2}$ minute, and serve.

Curried fried rice with shrimp

Preparation: 25 minutes + 2 hours standing and marinating time

1 cup peeled shrimp • salted water • 4 dried Chinese mushrooms • 1 small onion • 3 tbsp peas • 5 tbsp oil • 1 tbsp curry powder • 1 tbsp soy sauce • 1³/₄ lb cooked long-grain rice • ¹/₂ tbsp salt • pinch monosodium glutamate (optional)
For the seasoning: 1 tbsp saké or dry sherry • pinch salt • pinch monosodium glutamate (optional) • ¹/₂ tbsp cornstarch

1. Remove the black central nerve from the shrimp. Immerse the shrimp in salted water (1 tsp salt to 2 glasses water); let stand for 1 hour. Drain, dry the shrimp, and sprinkle with the seasoning ingredients. Marinate for 1 hour.

2. Meanwhile, soak the mushrooms for 30 minutes. Drain, discard the stems, and cut the caps and the onion into ¹/₄-in cubes. Cook the peas.

3. Heat 1 tbsp oil in the wok and stir-fry the shrimp until almost cooked. Transfer to a plate.

4. Heat 1 tbsp oil and sauté the mushrooms until they give off their aroma. Set aside.

5. Clean the wok, heat the remaining oil, and fry the onion for 1 minute. Lower the heat, fry the curry powder a little, add the mushrooms, and stir-fry. Dribble the soy sauce down the sides of the wok to the bottom. Let the aroma develop, add the rice, stir-fry a little, and season with salt and monosodium glutamate (if used).

6. Add the shrimp and peas. Mix thoroughly.

Five-color rice

Preparation: 25 minutes

3 dried Chinese mushrooms • 2 oz cooked ham • 4 oz lean pork • 1 leek • $^{1}/_{2}$ cup peeled shrimp • 2–3 tbsp peas • 2 eggs • salt • monosodium glutamate (optional) • $^{1}/_{3}$ cup oil • 2 tsp soy sauce • pinch pepper • $1^{3}/_{4}$ lb cooked long-grain rice

1. Soak the mushrooms in water for 30 minutes; drain and remove the stalks. Cut the mushroom caps, ham, and pork into $^1/_4$-in cubes. Chop the leek and shrimp. Lightly boil the peas and set aside.

2. Beat the eggs; season with a pinch of salt and monosodium glutamate (if used). Heat 1 tbsp oil in a wok. Stir-fry the eggs for 1 minute; set aside on a plate.

3. Heat 3 tbsp oil in the wok and stir-fry the mushrooms until cooked.

4. Add the pork and stir-fry, separating the pieces from one another, until the meat takes color. Add the shrimp and the ham.

5. Stir-fry briefly, pour in the soy sauce, let the aroma develop a little then season with the pepper and the monosodium glutamate (if used). Transfer the mixture to a plate.

6. Clean the wok. Heat 6 tbsp oil. Stir-fry the chopped leek without letting it burn for just long enough to flavor the oil.

7. Add the cooked rice; stir-fry over moderate heat, add salt to taste, and a pinch of monosodium glutamate (if used).

8. When the rice is well mixed with the oil, add the meat and shrimp mixture, stir-fry for a minute, then add the scrambled egg and the peas. Mix together and serve.

Tofu soup Peking style

Preparation: 30 minutes + soaking time

1–2 cakes tofu (bean curd) • 3 slices pork belly • 3 dried Chinese mushrooms • 5 Chinese leaves • gingko nuts to taste • ¹/₂ cup ground lean pork • 1 tbsp saké or dry sherry
For the sauce: 2 tbsp chopped leek • 1 tbsp grated root ginger • ¹/₃ tsp soy sauce • ¹/₃ tsp salt • 2 tbsp water • 2 tbsp cornstarch • pinch monosodium glutamate (optional) • pinch pepper
For the seasoning: 1 tbsp soy sauce • 1 tsp sugar • 1¹/₂ tsp salt • pinch monosodium glutamate (optional) • pinch pepper

1. Cut each tofu cake into 8 pieces; cut the pork belly into 2-in pieces. Soak the mushrooms for 30 minutes, discard the tough stems, quarter the caps, and cut each quarter in thin slices.

2. Cut the Chinese leaves in half lengthways then across in thin strips about 2 in long. Cut the strips in very fine slices. Shell the gingko nuts, boil the kernels in salted water, drain, and remove their thin skins.

3. Place the ground pork in a bowl with the sauce ingredients. Mix well, stirring until the meat reaches a soft doughy consistency.

4. Boil 1¹/₂ quarts water in a casserole. While the water is heating, shape the ground pork into balls 1 in wide. Drop the balls in the boiling water; add the mushrooms and pork belly and poach for 5 minutes. Mix the seasoning ingredients together then add to the water with the Chinese leaves.

5. When the leaves are tender adjust the seasoning if necessary; add the tofu, gingko nuts, and saké and boil for a minute longer.

6. Serve the soup piping hot.

Five-color soup

Preparation: 40 minutes

5 chicken wings • 10 quail's eggs • 3 tsp soy sauce • oil for frying • 10 scallops • 2 oz pork belly, cut in 3 slices • 3 dried Chinese mushrooms • 4 oz boiled bamboo shoots • 4 Chinese leaves • ½ medium-sized leek • 1 oz soy noodles • 1 tbsp peanut oil • 1 tbsp saké or dry sherry • 5 cups hot water • 1½ tsp salt • pinch monosodium glutamate (optional) • pinch pepper

1. Rinse the chicken wings and cut them in half. Place the quail's eggs with the chicken on a plate and put in a bamboo steamer. Steam for 5 minutes. Skin the meat and shell the eggs.

2. Sprinkle the wings and the eggs with 2 tsp soy sauce. Stir-fry in a pan with a little oil until a golden brown.

3. Clean and wash the scallops. Chop the pork belly.

4. Soak the mushrooms for 30 minutes. Discard the stems and slice the caps thinly. Thinly slice the bamboo shoots.

5. Cut the Chinese leaves in half lengthways, then across, in thin strips. Cut the leek in 1-in pieces.

6. Soften the noodles by pouring boiling water on them. Drain and cut into 4–5-in lengths.

7. Heat the peanut oil in a wok. Gently fry the leek; sprinkle on the remaining soy sauce and the saké. As soon as its aroma is released, add the boiling water.

8. Put the Chinese leaves in a casserole; distribute the rest of the ingredients on top, except for the scallops. Pour on the leek broth and season with salt and monosodium glutamate (if used).

9. Bring the broth back to a boil, lower the heat, and simmer until all the ingredients are just cooked. Finally, add the scallops and a pinch of pepper. Serve.

Yu ch'in
(Shark's fin soup)

Preparation: 2 hours 45 minutes

4 oz dried, cleaned shark's fin • 2 quarts basic chicken broth (see p. 9) • 2 shallots or slender leeks • 2 slivers root ginger • 3 dried Chinese mushrooms • 4 oz bamboo shoots • 2 tbsp peanut oil • 1 boneless chicken breast • 1 tbsp rice wine or saké • $1^1/_2$ tbsp soy sauce • 1 tbsp red wine vinegar • $^1/_2$ tsp sugar • $^1/_2$ tsp salt • 3 tbsp cornstarch

1. Boil the shark's fin in water for at least 2 hours, changing the water *every* 20 minutes. Use 2 pots, refilling alternately.

2. Rinse the shark's fin in cold water for 10 minutes; dry.

3. In a casserole bring to a boil the shallots and ginger with 3 cups broth, cover, and simmer for 15 minutes.

4. Soak the mushrooms in water for 30 minutes. Remove the stems and slice the caps thinly. Thinly slice the bamboo shoots.

5. Cut the chicken breast in slivers. Heat the oil in a clean casserole; lightly stir-fry the chicken slivers.

6. Add the remaining stock and bring to a boil. Add the bamboo shoots, mushrooms, rice wine, soy sauce, vinegar, sugar, and salt. Simmer slowly for 15–20 minutes.

7. Add the cornstarch diluted in 2 tbsp water. Stir occasionally to thicken the soup. Serve hot in small individual bowls, with added vinegar if wished.

Wonton soup

Preparation: 45 minutes + 4–5 hours standing time
including 30 minutes chilling time

1½ cups shrimp, chopped • 1 egg, beaten • 1 large leek or
scallion cut into thin rings
For the wontons: 1 cup all-purpose flour, sifted • 1 egg,
beaten with a little water • cornstarch
For the sauce: 1 tsp sugar • ½ tsp salt • ½ tsp monosodium
glutamate (optional) • 2–3 drops sesame seed oil
For the soup: 6¼ cups chicken broth (*see* p. 9) • 1 tsp salt •
½ tsp monosodium glutamate (optional) • 1½ tbsp light soy
sauce • 4–5 drops sesame seed oil

1. Make the wontons. (These may be prepared a day in advance if preferred.) Pour the flour on to a pastryboard and make a well in the center. Pour the egg and water mixture into the hollow. Mix to a smooth dough with a wooden spoon for about 5 minutes. Cover with a cloth and leave for 4–5 hours at room temperature.

2. Knead the dough lightly then roll into a paper-thin layer. Cut circles 3 in in diameter. Dust the circles with cornstarch and leave stacked in the refrigerator until needed.

3. Mix the sauce ingredients; amalgamate thoroughly with the shrimp. Refrigerate for 30 minutes.

4. Place 1 tsp shrimp mixture at the center of each wonton. Brush all round the edges with the egg mixture.

5. Fold and seal the wontons gently pressing the edges.

6. Bring a saucepan full of salted water to a boil. Plunge in the wontons. Cook for 2 minutes until the wontons rise to the surface, remove, and drain.

7. Place a few leek rings and wontons in 6 individual bowls.

8. Mix the soup ingredients and bring to a boil; add the remaining leek, simmer for 1 minute, pour into the bowls, and serve.

Huo kuo

Preparation: 45 minutes

14 oz ground lean pork • 1 egg • 1½ tbsp chopped leek • ½ tsp salt • pinch monosodium glutamate (optional) • pinch pepper • 5 dried Chinese mushrooms • oil for frying • few

drops peanut oil • 2 eggs, beaten • pinch salt • 5 tbsp cornstarch • 4–6 oz steamed white fish • 7 oz cleaned snails or oysters • 2 cakes fried tofu (bean curd) • 1 lb Chinese leaves • soy noodles to taste • gingko nuts to taste
For the sauce: mushroom water made up to 5½ cups with broth or hot water • 1 tbsp saké or dry sherry • 2 tsp salt • pinch pepper

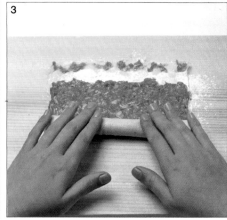

1. Put the pork in a bowl, add 1 egg, the chopped leek, salt, monosodium glutamate (if used), and pepper and mix well. Soak the mushrooms in water for 30 minutes.

2. Meanwhile, use three quarters of the meat mixture to shape 1-in balls. Heat enough oil for deep-frying until very hot. Plunge in the pork balls and immediately turn off the heat. After 3 minutes turn the heat on again. Continue cooking until the pork balls are well browned.

3. Beat 2 eggs well with a pinch of salt and 1 tsp cornstarch mixed with 1 tsp water. Heat the peanut oil in a small skillet and make a thin omelet. Spread the remaining meat mixture over the omelet; season with salt and a little monosodium glutamate (if used). Sprinkle with 4 tbsp cornstarch. Roll into a sausage, steam for 8 minutes, then cut into small slices.

4. Drain the mushrooms, reserving the water for the sauce. Discard the stems and slice the caps. Flake the white fish into small pieces. Rinse the snails or oysters. Blanch the fried tofu in boiling water for 1 minute.

5. Boil the Chinese leaves in salted water. Cut in 1½-in pieces. Pour boiling water over the noodles, cut in 5-in lengths. Boil the gingko nuts then remove the thin inner skin.

6. Line the hot pot with the Chinese leaves then arrange all the other ingredients in sections. Pour over the mushroom water and broth, saké, and salt and pepper. Heat through and serve.

Deep-fried sesame balls

Preparation: 1 hour

4 oz red soy powder • 1 lb sugar • 1½ tbsp pork fat • 5 oz rice flour • 3½ oz wheat flour • scant 3 oz white sesame seeds • oil for frying

1. Put the red soy powder in a pan; add 1 glass water and mix thoroughly with a wooden spatula. Cook gently for 5 minutes. Add the sugar, mix to a solid paste.

2. Refrigerate the red soy paste. Melt the pork fat in a pan or skillet; add the chilled soy paste; fry gently, stirring with a wooden spatula. When the flavor has developed, remove from the heat, cool, then refrigerate.

3. Put the rice flour in a bowl. Add the sifted wheat flour, mix thoroughly then gradually pour in 1 cup water, working it into the flour with your hands.

4. Make a stiff dough and shape into a large ball; roll on a pastryboard sprinkled with rice flour, into a stick 1 in in diameter.

5. Cut the dough in ¾-in slices (about 30). Lay the slices out one by one, pressing each one lightly with the palm of the hand.

6. Shape the chilled red soy paste into marble-sized balls, wrap each in a slice of dough and roll between your palms.

7. Spread the sesame seeds out on a flat dish. Roll the balls of dough over the seeds, pressing slightly so that the seeds stick evenly to the dough.

8. Heat plenty of oil in a pan or skillet to a low temperature. Immerse the balls with care. As soon as they float to the surface gradually raise the heat and deep-fry until a light golden brown.

Two-color lake

Preparation: 40 minutes

$1^{1}/_{4}$ tbsp sesame seeds • 4-5 tbsp corn meal • 4-5 tbsp sugar • $2^{1}/_{2}$ oz rice flour • red food coloring

1. Toast the sesame seeds, taking care that they do not scorch, then grind coarsely.

2. Sift the corn meal. Roast in a skillet over low heat for 15–20 minutes, stirring with a wooden spoon, until it turns color.

3. Add, little by little, 1 cup water, keeping the heat low. Stir in the sugar and keep stirring until a thick custard forms.

4. Add the ground sesame seeds, mix, set aside, and keep warm.

5. Place the rice flour in a bowl and add about $^{1}/_{3}$ cup water to make a thick paste.

6. Divide the paste in two. Add the red coloring to one part and mix with the paste until it is pale pink.

7. Shape the white and pink pastes into small balls about $^{1}/_{2}$ in in diameter. Cook in boiling water for 10–15 minutes.

8. Pour the custard into a deep serving dish, drop in the balls, and serve hot.

Almond jelly

Preparation: 1 hour 30 minutes

3 oz agar-agar • 3 cups water • 1 cup sugar • 1 cup milk •
$^1/_2$ tsp almond essence
For the fruit topping: $^1/_4$ melon • 4 peach halves in syrup •
2 tbsp sugar

1. Break the agar-agar into 2–3 pieces. Place in a bowl of water and soak for at least 1 hour, changing the water several times.

2. Gently squeeze the agar-agar to eliminate excess water then tear it into smaller pieces. Place in the amount of water indicated and cook over medium heat.

3. Melt the agar-agar completely stirring with a wooden spoon. (This process should be quick if the agar-agar was softened enough before cooking.) Add the sugar and stir until dissolved completely.

4. Add the milk and as soon as it begins to boil turn off the heat.

5. Add the almond essence, mix quickly, then strain the mixture through cheesecloth.

6. Rinse 4 dessert glasses in cold water, fill each glass two-thirds full with almond jelly, and put in the refrigerator to set. Purée the melon and peaches separately, adding a little sugar to each. Top the set almond jellies with the fruit purées and serve.

Fruit merry-go-round

Preparation: 1 hour 20 minutes

3 oz agar-agar • 3¹/₂ cups water • 1 cup sugar • juice of ¹/₂ lemon • few drops lemon essence • 1 small water melon • 1 can lychees

1. Break the agar-agar into 2–3 pieces and soak for 1 hour in several changes of cold water.

2. Gently squeeze the agar-agar to remove as much water as possible, place in a saucepan with the amount of water indicated, and heat.

3. When the agar-agar has completely melted add the sugar. When dissolved, turn off the heat, add the lemon essence, and stir.

4. Strain through cheesecloth.

5. Rinse a ring mold in cold water, quickly pour in the hot liquid, leave it to cool thoroughly, then place in the refrigerator to set.

6. Make small balls of melon with a melon scoop; drain the lychees. Chill both.

7. Just before serving unmold the jelly. Arrange the cold lychees and melon balls in the center and round the outside of the jelly ring.

Japan

Japanese culinary tradition is simpler and more refined than its Chinese counterpart. One major characteristic sets it apart: the esthetic quality is as important as flavor is to other cuisines. According to an old saying, food of the Land of the Rising Sun must be savored with the eye as well as the palate. The color combinations, shapes, the careful cutting and folding of ingredients recall the artistry of ikebana. Japanese cooks are unparalleled in the use of the knife, observing time-honored techniques whereby preparing a meal is nothing less than a ritual of esthetic creation. Soup, for example, should be very light, transparent, spangled with small, colored shapes; a rose of carrot, a delicate ring of leek, a diaphanous fan of cucumber. All cut, chiseled or folded with an eye for beauty and a flair for taste – food, literally, to nourish the soul as well as the body. Japanese cooking is also special in its close regard for nature. Dishes are seasonal, colors and flavors in intimate communion with the earth's cycle. The Japanese have traditionally lived on a marine and vegetarian diet. Most important are the soybean, imported from China in the eighth century and used in a thousand different ways, and fish, which is often eaten raw. Meat dishes however, are not altogether absent, such as "yakitori," chicken kabobs, and a kind of bourguignonne dip onomatopoeically named "shabu shabu," because of the murmuring noises it makes while cooking.

Fried chicken

Preparation: 30 minutes + 1 hour marinating time

1 chicken weighing 3 lb • 1 tsp grated root ginger • 3 tbsp soy sauce • 3 tbsp saké or dry sherry • all-purpose flour • oil for frying

1. Trim the fat and joint the chicken. Mix together the ginger, the soy sauce, and the saké in a shallow bowl and marinate the chicken pieces for 1 hour, stirring now and then.

2. Dry the chicken pieces well and dust with flour, shaking off any excess.

3. Heat plenty of oil in a skillet; put in the chicken a few pieces at a time.

4. Fry over medium heat until cooked through. (The cooking time will depend on the size of the different chicken pieces.)

5. When well browned and crisp, remove the chicken pieces with a slotted spoon and drain on kitchen towels before serving.

Chicken and egg casserole with rice

Preparation: 35 minutes

2 mushrooms • 7 oz boneless chicken thighs • 1 leek • 1 small onion • 1 cup *Niban dashi* (second stock) (see p. 9) • 2 tbsp saké or dry sherry • 3 tbsp light soy sauce • 1 tsp sugar • pinch salt • 4 eggs • boiled rice to serve

1. Clean and slice the mushrooms thinly. Cut the chicken thighs in strips, blanch for $1/2$ minute in boiling water, and drain. Finely slice the leek and onion.

2. Bring the stock to a boil in a casserole with the saké, soy sauce, and the sugar. Add the chicken, leek, onion, and mushrooms. Cook for 3–4 minutes. Check the seasoning.

3. Beat the eggs in a bowl. Pour the egg over the contents of the casserole. Stir the egg and cover.

4. After 2 minutes the egg should be soft, creamy, and lightly set but not enough so to be an omelet. Serve equal portions of chicken, mushroom, and egg in individual bowls with boiled rice.

Chicken yakitori

Preparation: 30 minutes + 30 minutes marinating time

2 lamb's or pig's kidneys • $^3/_4$ lb boneless chicken breasts • $^1/_2$ cup chicken livers • 2 green bell peppers • 2 onions • $^2/_3$ cup saké or dry sherry • $^2/_3$ cup soy sauce • 1 tbsp sugar • 1 tsp grated root ginger • pinch monosodium glutamate (optional) • oil

1. Cut the kidneys in half lengthways, remove the white sinew, and soak in cold water for a short while.

2. Cut the kidneys, chicken breasts, and livers into pieces about 1-in long. Remove the seeds and pith of the peppers and cut into 1-in pieces. Cut the onion in the same way.

3. Lightly oil some metal skewers. Thread the meat and vegetables alternately on to the skewers.

4. Place the saké, the soy sauce, sugar, ginger, and monosodium glutamate (if used) in a saucepan and bring to a boil. Place the kabobs in a baking tray or shallow dish; marinate with the boiled condiment liquid; after 15 minutes turn the kabobs and leave to marinate for a further 15 minutes.

5. Meanwhile, preheat the broiler or barbecue.

6. Broil the kabobs, turning them so that they cook evenly on all sides, and basting frequently with the marinade as they cook. Serve the yakitori immediately while still very hot.

Sukiyaki

Preparation: 45 minutes

1¼ lb fillet of beef • 8 mushrooms • 2 carrots • 8 leeks • 1 small head Chinese leaves • 7 oz tofu (bean curd) (optional) • 5 oz bamboo shoots • 8 French beans • 4 small cauliflower florets • 3½ oz soy noodles • 3 tbsp oil • 1 cup soy sauce • 1 cup saké or dry sherry • 2 tbsp sugar • 1½ cups chicken broth or water • 4 fresh eggs • 4 tbsp light soy sauce

1. Cut the meat into very fine slices. Wash and dry the mushrooms. Peel the carrots. Cut the carrots and leeks in diagonal slices. Wash the Chinese leaves. Cut the tofu into cubes.

2. Arrange the vegetables and meat on large plates. Space the slices of fillet to prevent them from sticking together.

3. Boil the noodles; when tender, freshen under running cold water. Drain and place with the vegetables.

4. Put prepared food on plates by a fondue burner. Set the table; use plates or individual bowls. and 4 side cups. Break an egg into each side cup, and beat lightly with a spoonful of light soy sauce.

5. Light the burner under a wide saucepan. Put the oil in the pan.

6. Mix together a quarter of the indicated quantity of soy sauce, saké, sugar, and broth. Pour in the saucepan, bring to a boil; lower the heat to a slow simmer and put in the ingredients starting with those that take longest to cook.

7. Replace reduced liquid as necessary with more soy sauce, saké, sugar, and stock.

8. Diners help themselves to a selection of the cooked ingredients, then dip the pieces in the raw egg and light soy sauce mixture.

Braised beef with rice

Preparation: 30 minutes

3 leeks • 2 tbsp oil • 7 oz lean beef, cut in very thin slices • 5 tbsp sugar • 2 tbsp saké or dry sherry • 5 tbsp soy sauce • 7 oz cellophane or rice stick noodles, softened in boiling water and chopped • 1 cake tofu (bean curd) • 2 tbsp mirin or sweet sherry • 6 dried Japanese mushrooms, soaked and boiled • 7 oz Chinese leaves or spinach • 2 eggs • 4 small bowls Japanese boiled rice (see p. 10)

1. Wash and slice the leeks (including the green part) and stir-fry in a heavy-bottomed saucepan with the oil.

2. Add the meat and stir-fry the slices to impregnate them with the leek juices.

3. When the meat is half cooked dilute 2 tbsp sugar with the saké and add to the saucepan. Cover and cook for 1 minute.

4. Add 2 tbsp soy sauce. Mix well. Cook for 2–3 minutes.

5. Add the noodles and the tofu, cut in cubes. Mix together 2 tbsp sugar, 2 tbsp soy sauce, and the mirin; pour into the saucepan. Add the softened mushrooms and the Chinese leaves, the remaining sugar, and soy sauce. Cook for a short while.

6. Finally pour in the beaten egg, stir, and cook for 2 minutes. Remove from the heat. Serve with boiled rice.

Shabu shabu (Japanese fondue)

Preparation: 1 hour 20 minutes

2 oz Chinese leaves • 2 oz spinach • 3 tbsp roasted and salted sesame seeds (goma shio) • 6¼ cups *Niban dashi* (second stock) (see p. 9) • 2 tbsp rice wine vinegar (su) or white wine vinegar • 2 tbsp soy sauce • 1 tbsp saké or dry sherry • pinch sugar • ½ tsp grated root ginger • ½ white radish (Daikon) • 1 dried chili pepper • 10½ oz tofu (bean curd) • 8 dried Chinese mushrooms • 3½ oz cellophane noodles • 1¼ lb fillet of beef • 1 onion • salt • pinch monosodium glutamate (optional)

1. Bring plenty of water to a boil in a large saucepan. Blanch the Chinese leaves for 30 seconds, remove, and drain. Blanch the spinach leaves for 1 minute, drain, and squeeze out the moisture.

2. Make a bed of Chinese leaves on a cloth; lay the dried spinach leaves on top in the center. Roll the Chinese and spinach leaves into a sausage shape.

3. Wrap the roll in the cloth and squeeze to expel any remaining liquid. Refrigerate for 1 hour. Unwrap the roll and cut into small rounds.

4. Grind the sesame seeds, place in a bowl, and mix with 2 tbsp stock, the vinegar, soy sauce, saké, sugar, and ginger. Set on the table.

5. Finely chop the white radish and the chili pepper; set on the table in a small bowl. Cut the tofu into cubes.

6. Soak the mushrooms for 30 minutes, dry, and discard the stalks. Boil the noodles and freshen with cold water when tender.

7. Cut the beef into very thin slices. Slice the onions. Arrange all the items on a platter and set on the table by the condiments.

8. Place a saucepan filled with boiling stock over a fondue burner in the middle of the table. Each person cooks their own selection of ingredients with a fondue fork in the simmering stock seasoned with a little salt and monosodium glutamate (if used). When done, the morsels are dipped in the condiment bowls, according to the flavor desired. At the end of the meal, the reduced stock is served as soup in individual bowls.

Sashimi (Raw fish)

Preparation: 30 minutes

1³/₄ lb very fresh assorted fish fillets (e.g. bream, sea bass, tuna, salmon, sole) • 1 carrot • 1 scallion • 1 small cucumber • 8 oz baby cuttlefish or squid • light soy sauce • Japanese horseradish paste or powder (*wasabi*)

1. Clean and dry the fish fillets and chill for a while in the coldest part of the refrigerator to make them easier to slice.

2. Prepare the vegetables. Peel, trim, and shred the carrot; trim the scallion and cut into thin rings; wash the cucumber and cut into wafer-thin diagonal slices.

3. Remove the fish from the refrigerator and cut in thinnish pieces about ¹/₃ in thick.

4. Prepare the cuttlefish or squid and slice in small strips. Make an attractive arrangement of fish and vegetables on individual plates.

5. Set a side bowl of soy sauce and a saucer of Japanese horseradish, to be diluted to taste by each plate on the table. If only powdered horseradish is available, make a sauce by mixing it with a little water. Dip the fish and the vegetables in either sauce before eating.

Fried fish with noodles

Preparation: 30 minutes

4 fresh medium-sized white fish • 2 oz buckwheat noodles • 2 sheets dried bean curd (yuba) or chopped *nori* seaweed • all-purpose flour • 3 egg whites • oil for frying • ¼ small squash • 1 bunch parsley
For the sauce (optional): 1 cup *Niban dashi* (second stock) (see p. 9) • ⅓ cup soy sauce • ⅓ tsp salt

1. Clean and gut the fish then wash and dry thoroughly. Cut and fillet as neatly as possible.

2. Cut the noodles in 1-in pieces.

3. Wrap the dried bean curd or *nori* in a cloth and crumble.

4. Dust the fish fillets, noodles, and curd crumbs with flour. Coat with egg white. Press firmly to make the noodles and crumbs stick to the fillets.

5. Heat plenty of oil in a saucepan to 350°F.

6. Fry the fillets until crisp and golden. Drain on kitchen towels.

7. Cut the squash in round slices. Make several small bunches of twisted parsley sprigs. Dust with flour, coat in egg white, and fry.

8. Serve, if wished, with a sauce made with the Japanese stock mixed with soy sauce and salt.

Marinated mackerel

Preparation: 50 minutes + 4 hours standing time

2 mackerel weighing approx. 1 lb each • salt • $^3/_4$ cup wine vinegar • 3 tbsp sugar • 6 tbsp light soy sauce • 3 tsp grated root ginger • 2 tbsp Japanese horse-radish powder (*wasabi*) • 2 carrots, cut into fine short matchsticks • 2 oz Japanese white radish (Daikon), cut into fine short matchsticks • 1 small bunch watercress (or parsley)

1. Trim, gut, and wash the fish. Fillet neatly, removing skin and bones. Cut into strips. Put in a bowl, sprinkle with salt, and refrigerate for 4 hours.

2. Dab the fish with a cloth to remove the salt. Return to the bowl, sprinkle with half the vinegar and 1$^1/_2$ tbsp sugar. Leave for 30 minutes.

3. Meanwhile, prepare the sauce. Bring to a boil in a saucepan the soy sauce with the remaining vinegar, 1 tbsp sugar, and the ginger. When the vinegar has evaporated a little turn off the heat and leave to cool. Pour the sauce into small individual bowls and place at the table.

4. Make a paste of green horseradish powder mixed with a little water. Place in a bowl on the table.

5. Remove the strips of fish from the marinating bowl and arrange them on a serving dish with the carrot and white radish sticks.

6. Decorate the dish with the watercress. Each person flavors their sauce to taste with the horseradish before dipping the fish in the sauce.

Tempura

Preparation: 1 hour

1 egg • 1 cup iced water • 1³/₄ cups all-purpose flour • ¹/₂ cup cornstarch • pinch salt • 12 asparagus tips • 12 French beans • 1 onion • 1 zucchini • 1 eggplant • 1 green bell pepper • 4 mushrooms • 8 large shrimp • 2¹/₄ cups *Niban dashi* (second stock) (see p. 9) • 2 tbsp light soy sauce • 2 tbsp mirin or sweet sherry • oil for frying.

1. Make a batter by whisking the egg with the iced water, then gradually adding the sifted flour and cornstarch and finally the salt. Do not over-beat; the mixture must be smooth but not too dense. Refrigerate for 1 hour.

2. Wash, trim, and dry all the vegetables and cut into thin slices (use the mushroom caps only). Cut the fish fillets into bite-sized pieces.

3. Clean and shell the shrimp but leave the tail shell on. Remove the head and black vein. Arrange the shrimp, fish, and vegetables on a large plate and refrigerate.

4. Pour the stock, soy sauce, and mirin into a saucepan, stir thoroughly, and heat to a simmer. Cook for 1 minute then pour the sauce into individual small bowls, one for each place setting.

5. Pour plenty of oil into a large saucepan or skillet and heat to 350°F. Remove the batter from the refrigerator. Dip the ingredients in the chilled batter and deep-fry.

6. Keep the temperature of the oil steady. The cooking time for each ingredient will vary. (The fish should be a golden color all over.) Each person dips the hot morsels in the sauce before eating. Other vegetables, prepared in the same way, can be used in this dish if preferred.

Fish rolls

Preparation: 1 hour + 40 minutes standing time

14 oz silver mullet • salt • wine vinegar • sugar • 2 eggs •
$^{1}/_{2}$ tsp cornstarch • $^{1}/_{2}$ tsp saké • sesame seed oil • 1 small
piece carrot • 1 $^{3}/_{4}$-in piece root ginger • 1 cucumber

1. Gut the fish, remove its head, and cut in half lengthways.

2. Lay the fish halves on a plate or board, sprinkle with salt and set aside for 40 minutes.

3. Skin and fillet the fish, starting from the head end. Make sure no bones remain. Place the fillets in a saucepan with 3 tbsp vinegar mixed with 2 tsp sugar and salt, and cook over low heat.

4. Beat the egg, cornstarch and saké and strain through cheesecloth.

5. Grease a saucepan or skillet lightly with oil and fry 2 small omelets.

6. Shred the carrot, sprinkle with salt, and squeeze dry. Marinate in 3 tbsp vinegar, 1 tbsp sugar and a pinch of salt. Cut the ginger in strips.

7. Using a sharp knife, peel a long, fine spiral of cucumber skin. Soak for 2 minutes in $2^{1}/_{2}$ cups water, drain thoroughly and cut in half.

8. Lay the 2 omelets on a bamboo mat. Spread each with a half fish, carrot, and ginger. Roll into cylinders, wrap firmly in cucumber peel, leave to stand for 10 minutes, then slice.

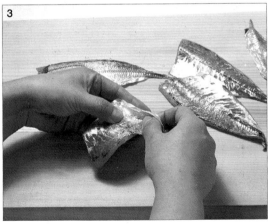

Scallops with scallions

Preparation: 30 minutes

12 scallions • salt • 12 scallops • 3 leaves *wakame* seaweed • 4 tbsp white fermented soy paste • 4 tbsp *Niban dashi* (second stock) (*see* p. 9) • 1 tbsp rice wine vinegar (su) or white wine vinegar

1. Trim and wash the scallions, boil them in lightly salted water for 5 minutes and immediately freshen under running cold water. Drain well.

2. Boil a little water in a separate saucepan and simmer the scallops for 5 minutes. Drain and dry on kitchen towels.

3. Soak the seaweed in a pot of water for 10 minutes.

4. Meanwhile, cut the scallions into 1-in pieces and slice the scallops horizontally in half.

5. Mix the soy paste into the stock and vinegar. Bring the mixture to a boil in a small saucepan. Simmer for 3 minutes, stirring continuously.

6. Drain the seaweed, slice it into thin strips and place in a serving bowl with the scallions and the scallops.

7. Pour over the sauce and wait for it to cool, stirring from time to time, before serving at room temperature.

Rolled omelet with spinach

Preparation: 40 minutes

¾ lb fresh spinach • 1 tsp salt • 3 eggs • 1 tbsp light soy sauce • 1 tsp sugar • peanut or olive oil

1. Trim and thoroughly wash the spinach; place still wet in a saucepan with a little salt and cook for 5 minutes, uncovered. Drain, squeeze out all the moisture, and divide it into two lots.

2. Beat the eggs with a fork adding the soy sauce, sugar, and a small pinch of salt. Oil and heat a 9-in nonstick skillet and pour in half of the egg mixture. Make a thin omelet and remove from the heat while the surface is still creamy.

3. Spread half of the spinach on the omelet applying a little pressure to make it adhere to the soft egg surface.

4. Roll up the omelet with the help of a spatula and form a neat cylinder.

5. Return the skillet to the heat and brown the omelet roll lightly on both sides. Remove from the skillet and wrap in waxed paper to hold the roll in shape. Set aside to cool. Oil the skillet again and repeat the process with the remaining egg and spinach.

6. When the two omelet rolls are completely cold, remove the wrapping and slice. Arrange the slices on a serving dish and serve cold.

71

Oden
(Vegetable casserole)

Preparation: 1 hour 45 minutes

9 oz *konnyaku* • salt • 2 carrots • 3½ oz Japanese white radish (Daikon) or turnip • 8 slices frozen deep-fried tofu (*atsu age*) • 2 pieces frozen white fish cake (*sazuma age*) • 1 tbsp instant Japanese stock (*dashi no moto*, see p. 9) • 1 piece *kombu* seaweed (kelp) • 1 tsp sugar • 2 tbsp soy sauce • 3 tbsp mirin or saké • 4 cabbage leaves • 10½ oz tofu (bean curd)

1. Wash the *konnyaku* in cold water; dry, sprinkle with a little salt, and cut into squares. Scrape the carrot and white radish and cut into large rounds.

2. Pour boiling water over the fried tofu and fish cake to thaw.

3. Dissolve the instant stock in 4½ cups hot water. Do not boil.

4. Add the seaweed, sugar, soy sauce, mirin, and a little salt. Simmer for a minute, add the carrot and radish and simmer for a further 10 minutes. (Do not fully boil or the flavor of the stock will spoil.)

5. Add separately, without mixing, the cabbage leaves, the *konnyaku* and the softened fried tofu, and fish cake. Simmer for 30 minutes.

6. Lastly add the tofu, cut into cubes, and simmer for a further 30 minutes.

7. Divide the vegetables equally in individual serving bowls. (If fried tofu and *sazuma age* fish cake are not available, substitute with onion-flavored meatballs bound with flour and egg and fried in oil before being added to the saucepan with the other ingredients.) Other vegetables may be added to taste, e.g. leeks and mushrooms. Oden may be served with boiled rice.

Carrots and konnyaku with tofu

Preparation: 50 minutes

3 pieces *konnyaku* • 3 carrots • 1 cake tofu (bean curd) • 1 cup *Niban dashi* (second stock) (*see* p. 9) • 1 tsp sugar • 1 tsp salt • 5 tbsp roasted sesame seeds • 2 tbsp light soy sauce • 1 sprig parsley (optional)

1. Parboil the *konnyaku* in boiling water. Drain and cut lengthways in $^1/_4$-in slices.

2. Scrape, wash, and cut the carrots into small sticks.

3. Place the tofu in a sieve and leave to drain thoroughly.

4. Pour the stock into a saucepan, add the *konnyaku* and the carrot, bring to boiling point, and leave to cool.

5. When cold remove and drain the *konnyaku* and carrot and place in a salad bowl.

6. Sieve the tofu into a bowl and add the sugar, salt, sesame seeds, and soy sauce. Mix well and add to the contents of the salad bowl. Mix the ingredients very gently and lightly together and decorate with the sprig of parsley if wished.

Crab and cucumber salad

Preparation: 20 minutes

1 cucumber • salt • 7 oz fresh or canned crabmeat • 5 tbsp white wine vinegar • 1 tsp sugar • 1 tbsp sesame seeds

1. Wash, dry, and trim the cucumber and cut into very thin, oblique rounds. Place in a bowl, sprinkle with a little salt, and set aside for a few minutes.

2. Flake the crabmeat with a fork.

3. Mix the vinegar, sugar, and salt in a bowl. Make sure that the sugar has completely dissolved.

4. Rinse the cucumber slices, dry on kitchen towels, and place in a bowl.

5. Add the crabmeat and pour on the vinegar dressing.

6. Mix well and sprinkle with the sesame seeds.

Roasted eggplants with sesame seeds

Preparation: 40 minutes

2 large eggplants • 2 tsp sesame seeds • 1 tbsp Japanese horseradish powder (*wasabi*) • 6 tbsp light soy sauce

1. Heat the oven to 475°F. Wash and dry the eggplants. Leave whole.

2. Roast the eggplants directly on a rack in the middle of the oven, turning them occasionally to cook evenly on all sides. Remove after about 30 minutes and leave to cool a little.

3. Peel the eggplants – the skin will come away quite easily – and cut into 4 slices.

4. Roast the sesame seeds in a nonstick saucepan; remove from the heat as soon as they start leaping in the saucepan; crush with the flat end of a knife blade and sprinkle over the eggplant pieces.

5. Dissolve the powdered radish in a little cold water and place in a small bowl. Set at the table.

6. Distribute the soy sauce in 4 little bowls and set them at the table. Add a little horseradish to each bowl of soy sauce and dip the eggplant pieces into this relish before eating.

Rice rolls

Preparation: 3 hours 30 minutes

3–4 dried Japanese mushrooms (*shiitake*) • approx. 7 tbsp sugar • 5 tbsp mirin • 5 tbsp soy sauce • salt • dried melon pulp • 1 cup *Niban dashi* (second stock) (see p. 9) • 3 eggs • 1³/₄ lb Japanese boiled rice (see p. 9) • 3 tbsp white wine vinegar • 1 cod steak • red food coloring • 6 sheets *nori* seaweed • 3¹/₂ oz spinach leaves

Preliminary preparations: soak the mushrooms for 20 minutes, drain, and reserve the water. Boil in $^2/_3$ cup mushroom water mixed with 2 tbsp sugar, 2 tbsp mirin and 2 tbsp soy sauce. Drain and cut into strips.

Wash the melon pulp, rub with salt, and soak for 2 hours. Wash again and cook in the stock until soft. Add 2 tbsp sugar, 2 tbsp mirin and 2 tbsp soy sauce; continue cooking over low heat.

Make an omelet with the beaten eggs mixed with 2 tsp sugar and pinch salt. Make a dressing of vinegar, 1 tbsp sugar, 1 tbsp mirin, and 1 tbsp salt. Mix into the boiled rice.

Steam the cod, remove the skin, pulp the flesh, and add a little red food coloring.

1. For 1 large roll use $1^1/_2$ sheets seaweed stuck together with boiled rice and laid flat on a bamboo mat or teacloth.

2. Spread a layer of the seasoned rice on the seaweed up to $^1/_8$-in from the edge.

3. Make 4 long furrows in the rice.

4. Distribute one quarter each of the melon, boiled spinach, mushrooms, omelet, and fish along the furrows.

5. Lift the front of the mat or cloth to help you start rolling the ingredients.

6. Continue rolling and use pressure to make the roll compact.

7. Close the ends of the mat and set aside. Prepare 3 more rolls in the same way.

8. Just before serving, tidy the edges of the rolls with a knife, take them out of the mats or cloth, and cut into thick slices.

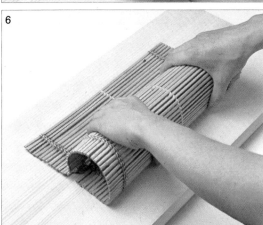

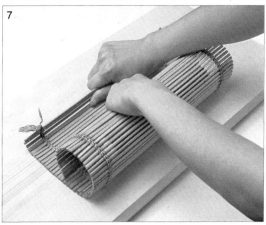

Red rice

Preparation: 2 hours 30 minutes

2¹/₄ lb aduki beans (red soybeans) • 5 cups glutinous rice soaked overnight in water • sesame salt

1. Cook the aduki beans in plenty of boiling water for 15 minutes, taking care that their skins do not break. Drain the beans.

2. Return the beans to the saucepan. Cook in plenty of water over moderate heat for about 1–1¹/₂ hours or until tender, keeping the beans submerged with the aid of a lid floating on the surface of the water.

3. Drain the beans and reserve the cooking water.

4. Stir the bean water and scoop it up in the air with a ladle.

5. This action will speed up the cooling process and enhance the color of the bean water.

6. Drain the rice thoroughly. Spread a napkin over a bamboo steamer, put the rice in it, distributed evenly, and make a hollow in the middle for the aduki beans. Steam the rice, using the bean water, for 30–40 minutes, sprinkling now and then with hot water seasoned with sesame salt.

79

Nigiri sushi (rice balls with fish)

Preparation: 40 minutes

4 eggs ● oil ● 10$\frac{1}{2}$ oz assorted fish fillets (*e.g.* tuna, salmon, bream, sole, etc) ● 4 shrimp ● 1 lb Japanese boiled rice (p. 9) ● 3 tbsp white wine vinegar ● 1 tbsp sugar ● 1 tbsp mirin ● 1 tbsp salt ● few strips pickled ginger ● light soy sauce ● Japanese horseradish paste or powder (*wasabi*)

1. Beat the eggs lightly with a fork and cook 2 thin omelets with a little oil in a cast-iron skillet. Leave to cool and cut in 2-in strips.

2. Slice the fish fillets in fine strips like the omelet. Peel and cut the shrimp in half lengthways. Mix the vinegar, sugar, mirin, and salt into the rice.

3. Wet your hands and make rice balls, slightly oval in shape and about 2$\frac{1}{2}$-in long. Place each ball directly on to a large serving dish.

4. Place on each ball a strip of ginger covered with a strip of fish or omelet or half a shrimp. When the serving dish is full place it in the center of the table.

5. Fill small bowls with a little light soy sauce and put by each place setting. Also lay at the table a small plate of horseradish paste. If powder is used add a few drops of water to make a paste.

6. Flavor the soy sauce with the horseradish paste according to personal taste (try only a little paste at first because it is very hot). Dip the garnished rice balls in the sauce before eating.

Cold noodles with soy sauce

Preparation: 15 minutes + 1 hour chilling time

1 lb buckwheat noodles • $^2/_3$ cup light soy sauce • 3 tbsp saké or dry sherry • 1 tsp sugar • 2 tomatoes • 1 leek • 1 tsp grated root ginger

1. Cook or soak the noodles in plenty of boiling water according to the manufacturer's instructions. Drain when almost tender, cool under running water, place in an earthenware dish, and refrigerate for about 1 hour.

2. Meanwhile pour the soy sauce, the saké, and the sugar in a saucepan, bring to a boil and simmer for a few minutes to reduce a little. Pour into a container and cool. When cold, chill in the refrigerator.

3. Just before serving, cut the tomatoes in segments and slice the leek into thin rings.

4. Divide the cold noodles equally in 4 shallow bowls. Garnish with the tomatoes, the leek, and the ginger. Provide each person with a small bowl of the sauce as a dip for the noodles before they are eaten.

Tofu and miso soup

Preparation: 20 minutes

1 cake tofu (bean curd) • green tips of 2 scallions • 4$^{1}/_{2}$ cups Japanese stock (*see* p. 9) • 7 oz white fermented soy paste (*miso*)

1. Cut the tofu into $^{1}/_{2}$-in cubes. Wash the green scallion tips and cut into fine rings.

2. Bring the stock to a boil in a saucepan.

3. Dilute the *miso* in a little of the stock (about 1 cup) and pour back into the saucepan.

4. While bringing back to a boil add the tofu cubes and cook for 1 minute. Turn off the heat, cover, and leave for a minute or two. Pour the soup into bowls, add the scallion rings, and serve.

Pork and tomato soup

Preparation: 20 minutes + 20 minutes marinating time

$3^1/_2$ oz lean pork • 1 tsp light soy sauce • 1 tsp saké • 2 ripe tomatoes • 1 small onion • 2 tbsp oil • salt • $4^1/_2$ cups meat broth • pepper • 1 egg • 1 small sprig coriander

1. Cut the pork into small pieces, add the soy sauce and the saké, and leave to marinate for 20 minutes.

2. Meanwhile, wash, dry, and chop the tomato. Peel and finely chop the onion.

3. Heat the oil in a large saucepan. Fry the onion until golden brown, add the meat, and cook for a few minutes. Add the chopped tomato, pour in the broth, and season with salt and pepper. Continue cooking over low heat.

4. Break the egg into a bowl and beat it with a fork. When the meat is tender, add the egg to the soup. Serve the soup piping hot with a sprinkling of chopped coriander leaves on top.

Shrimp and vegetable soup

Preparation: 1 hour 30 minutes

Salt • 3¹/₂ oz soy noodles • 4 dried Japanese mushrooms (*shiitake*) • 4 snow peas • 2 carrots • 3¹/₂ oz Chinese leaves • 4 mint leaves • 1 oz root ginger • 2 oz Japanese white radish (Daikon) • ¹/₂ cup cooked, peeled shrimp • 4 scallions • 2¹/₂ cups Japanese stock (see p. 9) • pinch monosodium glutamate (optional)

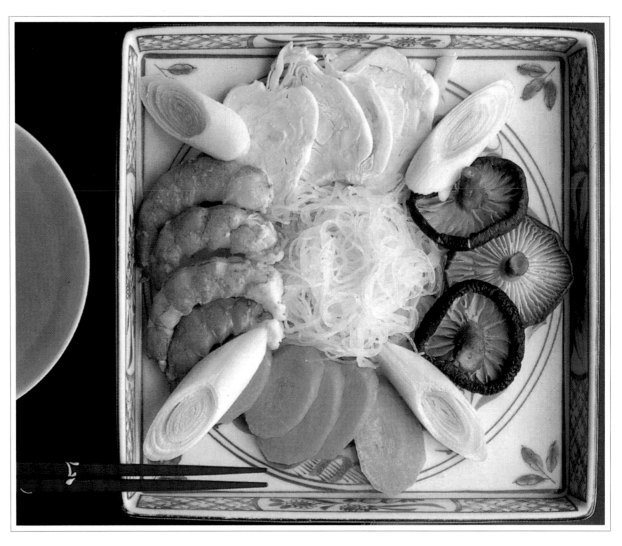

1. Bring plenty of salted water to a boil. Cook the noodles for 30 minutes over low heat.

2. Meanwhile, soak the mushrooms in lukewarm water for 30 minutes. Place in a pot with enough water to cover and simmer for 20 minutes.

3. Clean and trim the snow peas, boil for 5 minutes, and drain. Peel, wash, and slice the carrots. Wash the Chinese leaves and cut into ³/₄-in slices. Wash and dry the mint. Peel and grate the ginger. Wash and finely chop or shred the radish. Trim, wash, and diagonally slice the scallion.

4. Drain the noodles. Drain the mushrooms with a sieve and save the water. Lay all the ingredients decoratively on a large serving dish except for the ginger and the radish and place these separately on two small plates.

5. Pour the mushroom water into the stock, bring to a boil, add the monosodium glutamate (if used), and cook for a few minutes. Remove from the heat.

6. Pour the soup into small bowls. Serve the vegetables separately, seasoning to taste with the ginger or radish.

Egg and noodle soup

Preparation: 25 minutes

4¹/₂ cups Japanese stock (*see* p. 9) • 7 oz wide ribbon noodles • 2 scallions • 3¹/₂ oz spinach • 1 carrot • 2 small mushrooms • 1 tbsp soy sauce • 4 eggs • pinch sugar • salt

1. Bring the stock to a boil, add the noodles, and cook until almost tender.

2. Meanwhile, slice the scallions into thin rings. Cook the spinach and the carrot; slice the carrot; blanch the mushrooms.

3. When the noodles are ready, add the spinach, carrot, the blanched mushrooms, scallion, soy sauce, and the sugar. Add salt to taste.

4. Fill 4 bowls with the soup. Carefully break an egg into each bowl and cover for 2 minutes to allow the egg to set a little. Serve immediately.

85

Dango
(rice flour balls)

Preparation: 1 hour

For the dough: 2 cups rice flour • 1 cup lukewarm water
For the sauce: 3 tbsp sugar • 3 tbsp water • 3 tbsp soy sauce
• 1 heaping tbsp cornstarch

1. Blend the rice flour with the water until the consistency is smooth and elastic.

2. Soak a small clean cloth in water, squeeze well, and spread over the bottom of a bamboo steamer. Coarsely break the dough into pieces with your hands and place in the steamer. Steam over brisk heat for 20–30 minutes.

3. Remove from the heat and immediately pound the dough with a wooden pestle. Divide the resulting pulp in 2 and make 2 small cylinders ³/₄ in thick.

4. Plunge the cylinders in iced water for a few minutes to firm them. Pat dry with a cloth then cut in ³/₄-in slices and roll these into small balls with the hands.

5. Wet some skewers and thread 4–5 balls onto each.

6. Mix the sauce ingredients together and cook in a small saucepan until thickened.

7. Lightly sear the little balls all over under a heated broiler.

8. Lay them on a plate and pour on the sauce.

Sweet potato tartlets with chestnut

Preparation: 1 hour

7 oz sweet potatoes • 6 tbsp sugar • $\frac{1}{2}$ tsp salt • 1 tsp powdered green tea • 8 chestnut halves or 8 small whole chestnuts (roasted, peeled, and boiled in sweetened milk until tender) or 4 marrons glacés cut in half

1. Wash and peel the sweet potatoes. Slice into $\frac{3}{4}$-in pieces. Leave in water for 30 minutes to reduce the acidity.

2. Boil the potato slices in plenty of fresh water until tender.

3. Drain and while still hot work the potato through a sieve with a wooden spatula.

4. Place the mashed potatoes in a casserole over low heat with the sugar. Stir continuously until at boiling point, add the salt, give one more stir, and remove from the heat. Cool completely.

5. Form 9 equal potato balls, kneading one of them together with the green tea powder (use a few drops of water for extra malleability, if necessary). Cover your palm with a damp cloth; slide 1 pale ball on to the cloth and attach to it $\frac{1}{8}$ piece of the green ball.

6. Fold an edge of the cloth over the ball; flatten and form a disk 4 in in diameter, with the green patch on the underside near the perimeter.

7. Place 1 chestnut half in the middle of the disk.

8. Still using the cloth, close the disk around the chestnut to form a tartlet. Repeat steps 5 to 8 with the remaining balls.

Fruit jelly

Preparation: 1 hour + 5 hours soaking time + setting time

1 strip agar-agar • $1^{1}/_{4}$ cups cold water • $1^{1}/_{4}$ cups sugar • 2 egg whites • 7 oz strawberries of equal size

1. Cut the agar-agar into little pieces with scissors. Soak in the water for at least 5 hours. Bring the agar-agar slowly to a boil using the same water. Continue at simmering temperature until the threads of agar-agar have completely dissolved.

2. Add the sugar, stir, remove from the heat, and leave to cool.

3. Whisk the egg whites until firm. Add the cold mixture little by little and continue whisking until fully amalgamated.

4. Rinse a shallow rectangular dish under running cold water and pour the jelly into it. Drop in the strawberries carefully, one by one. Allow the jelly to set then cut into squares.

Fruit meringue

Preparation: 45 minutes

2 red dessert apples • 2 ripe bananas • 2 tbsp butter • 1 lemon • 2 eggs • 1 cup confectioner's sugar • 3 tbsp milk • 3 tbsp cornstarch

1. Peel and core the apples, leaving them whole. Cut into thin rings. Peel the bananas and slice into rounds.

2. Lightly butter a round cake pan. Carefully arrange alternate layers of apple and banana, starting with the apple. Sprinkle each layer with a few drops of lemon juice.

3. Preheat the oven to 425°F. Separate the eggs. Put the yolks in a basin with half the sugar, the milk, and the cornstarch. Add 2 tbsp water and beat with a whisk.

4. Pour into a heavy-based saucepan. Heat very slowly until the mixture thickens a little, then pour over the fruit.

5. Whisk the egg whites with the remaining sugar until stiff. Spread over the custard and fruit. Place in the oven for 15 minutes or until the top of the meringue is golden brown. This dessert is delicious eaten hot or cold.

Japanese sweetmeats

Preparation: 1 hour 30 minutes

¹/₂ cup aduki beans (red soy beans) • 1¹/₄ cups sugar • salt •
1 cup short-grain rice
For the coating: 2 tbsp soy flour mixed with 2 tbsp sugar and
a pinch of salt • 4 tbsp sesame seeds, roasted and coarsely
ground, mixed with 2 tbsp sugar and a pinch of salt

1. Boil the aduki beans in sufficient water to cover for about 1 hour.

2. While the beans are cooking skim any scum from the surface and replenish the water whenever necessary.

3. Drain, stir in the sugar, and heat in a heavy-based saucepan until all the moisture has evaporated. Add ¹/₂ tsp salt and mix well.

4. Transfer to a large bowl and leave to cool.

5. Cook the rice in salted water. Drain thoroughly, leave for a few minutes then pound with a wooden pestle.

6. Make 20 small rice balls and the same amount using the beans. Cover your hand with a damp cloth. Lay a ball of the bean mixture on the palm and flatten it into the shape of a disk. Place a ball of rice in the middle, wrap the cloth around, and reshape the bean mixture into a ball. Make 20 similar red-coloured balls, leave one third as they are, and coat one third with the soy flour and the remaining third with the ground sesame seeds.

Misuyokan

Preparation: 2 hours

1¹/₄ cups aduki beans ● 1¹/₂ cups sugar ● ¹/₂ tsp salt ● 1 strip agar-agar ● 3 glasses water

1. Cook the aduki beans following steps 1 and 2 of the recipe for Japanese Sweetmeats on p. 90. Mash the beans and pass through a sieve.

2. Put the resulting bean pulp into a cloth bag and squeeze thoroughly to leave the pulp as dry as possible.

3. Gently heat the pulp in a heavy-based saucepan over very low heat together with 1¹/₄ cups sugar and the salt. Stir until the consistency is such that it no longer sticks to the saucepan or the spatula.

4. Reconstitute the agar-agar in water for 30 minutes. Squeeze well with a cloth then dissolve completely over medium heat in the water.

5. Add the remaining sugar; when it has dissolved remove from the heat and pass the jelly liquid through a sieve lined with a damp cloth.

6. Return to the heat and add the bean paste in small amounts, stirring constantly. When the mixture starts to boil, lower the heat and cook for another 2–3 minutes.

7. Cool the mixture by placing the saucepan in a bowl of iced water. Continue stirring.

8. Pour into a square cake pan or mold. Leave to set at room temperature. Turn out and cut into shapes as desired.

India

According to an old Indian legend, rice sprang miraculously from the tomb of a young maiden whose last wish to the god Shiva was for something good and healthy to eat that one would never tire of. Shiva, for love of the child, gave the world the rice plant; ever since, it has been the "sustenance and delight" of the Indian people and one of the few but important common denominators of their composite gastronomy. Another common factor in Indian cooking is the fondness for spices, widely used for their color and flavor. The most representative is curry, not the powdered concoction that passes for curry in the West but an aromatic condiment obtained by patiently mixing pepper, cardamom, cloves, cinnamon, and other spices in accordance with ancient tradition. Curry is used to flavor a number of foods, from rice and lamb to chicken, fish, and vegetables. Another aspect of Indian cuisine is the length of the cooking time. Pleasant as the food is, to the Western palate it often seems overcooked. The long cooking process is further drawn out by the laborious preparation of some of the traditional dishes. Not for nothing is patience regarded as an essential quality of the good Indian cook. At table, dishes are served all at once, and each person makes his or her own selection. The sweet and sour flavors are a perfect foil for the hot ingredients and even the most unlikely combinations usually make good eating. Bread and rice are the normal accompaniments and dishes often arrive at table arranged in clusters on round tin or pewter trays called *thali*. The bright colors of the ingredients served in this way are evocative of the vivid folk culture of the Indian subcontinent.

Chapatis (unleavened bread rounds)

Preparation: 45 minutes + 2 hours standing time

2 cups wholemeal flour • 1 tsp salt • lukewarm water • extra flour for working with the dough

1. Sieve the flour on to a board and make a well in the middle. Add the salt and a little lukewarm water at a time, working in the flour with the hands. The exact amount of water will depend on the type of flour used. About $^1/_2$ cup is usually sufficient.

2. Knead the dough until it is smooth and elastic. Place in a bowl covered with a cloth and leave to stand for 2 hours.

3. Flour your hands and divide the dough into 8 parts. Shape each part into a small ball with your palms.

4. Use a rolling pin to form thin disks about $5^1/_2$ in in diameter.

5. Cover the bottom of a cast-iron saucepan or skillet with a very light sprinkling of flour and place on the heat. Make the chapatis one at a time; gently lower 1 disk into the saucepan, cook on one side for 1 minute, then turn with a spatula and cook the other side.

6. Draw the saucepan off the heat, lift out the chapati with kitchen tongs, and hold directly over low heat, watching that it does not burn. When a slight bubbling and swelling occur, and dark spots appear on the surface, the chapati is ready. Once swollen, the chapatis are pricked with a fork and eaten straight away or, more often, transferred directly on to a heated plate and wrapped in a cloth, or kept warm in a slow oven until ready to eat.

Naan (leavened bread)

Preparation: 1 hour + 2 hours standing time

3 cups all-purpose flour • 1 tsp salt • ¹/₂ cup plain yoghurt • ¹/₂ cup milk • 1 tsp sugar • 1 tsp dried yeast • 1 tbsp poppy seeds • ¹/₄ cup ghee (see p. 9)

1. Sieve the flour into a large basin, add the salt and the yoghurt, and amalgamate thoroughly with the help of a little water if necessary.

2. Warm the milk, dissolve the sugar and the yeast, and work in the flour and yoghurt mixture.

3. Knead the dough, adding water or flour depending on whether the consistency is too hard or too soft.

4. Continue kneading and pounding for about 15 minutes. Return the dough to the basin, cover with a damp cloth, and leave for 2 hours in a warm place after which it should have risen to twice its size.

5. When risen, break off a part of the dough equal to a ball of 2–2¹/₂ in in diameter. Shape it with your hands into an oval of about 2¹/₂–3 in long and 1¹/₂–2 in wide. Repeat the process until the dough is used up and lay the naan on an oven tray lightly greased with ghee.

6. Heat the oven to 400°F. Place the poppy seeds in a bowl and, with wet fingers, spread the seeds on the top of each naan pressing lightly to make them stick. Brush over with melted ghee and bake for 10 minutes until they are nicely rounded and have turned a honey gold color. Serve immediately, keeping warm under a cloth.

Samosas

Preparation: 1 hour 30 minutes

2 cups wholemeal flour • pinch salt • $\frac{1}{3}$ cup shortening • 1 cup fresh milk • 6 tbsp oil for frying
For the filling: $2\frac{1}{4}$ lb potatoes • salt • 1 tsp curry powder • 1 tsp cumin seeds • 2 cloves garlic • 4 fresh chili peppers • $\frac{1}{2}$ cup sunflower oil • 1 tbsp chopped parsley

1. Mix the flour with the salt on a pastryboard. Add the shortening in small pieces and work in the flour. Make a hollow in the middle and add the milk little by little working it in until the dough is smooth and homogeneous. Set aside in a cool place.

2. Prepare the filling. Peel the potatoes and cook in salted water flavored with the curry. Drain and dice.

3. Crush the cumin seeds, the garlic, and the chilis and sauté in a skillet with the oil; add the potatoes and fry, stirring, for 5 minutes over very low heat. Set aside to cool then sprinkle with the parsley.

4. Make small balls with the dough and roll them into thin circles about 7 in in diameter. Cut these in half and fold into cones, sealing the edge with a moistened finger.

5. Put a little of the potato filling into each cone, press the top edges together, and seal with a little water.

6. Heat the frying oil and fry the samosas until crisp and golden.

Parathas (butter-fried griddle bread)

1½ cups all-purpose flour • 1½ cups wholemeal flour • 1 tsp salt • 1 cup water • ½ cup ghee (see p. 9)

Preparation: 1 hour + 3 hours standing time

1. Sieve the flours and salt into a large basin. Add the water a little at a time and work in the flour until it becomes a fairly stiff dough. Cover with a cloth and leave in a cool place for 3 hours.

2. Divide the dough into 12 balls. Lightly flour a cool surface and roll each ball into a circle about ¼ in thick.

3. Melt the ghee and brush some lightly over the dough circles.

4. Fold the circles in half, brush with ghee again, turn over, and brush the other half.

5. Unfold and repeat steps 3 and 4 so that each circle gets fully impregnated with ghee. Parathas are prepared round or folded in triangles, rolled ¼ in thick.

6. Fry the parathas on both sides in hot ghee and serve while still hot.

Banana fritters

Preparation: 45 minutes

1 tbsp ghee (*see p. 9*) • 1 large, ripe banana (other fruits, e.g. mango or apple, can be substituted) • 2$^{1}/_{2}$ cups all-purpose flour • 1 tbsp sugar • 1 tsp salt • 1 tsp nigella seeds (kalongi) • oil for frying

1. Prepare the ghee in advance. Peel and purée the banana (or alternative fruit chosen).

2. Sieve 2$^{1}/_{4}$ cups of the flour on to a pastry board. Make a hollow in the middle and put in the sugar, the salt, the nigella seeds, the fruit purée, and the ghee.

3. Work in the flour with your hands adding enough water to make a smooth and elastic dough. Form into a ball.

4. Roll out strips of dough about $^{1}/_{8}$ in thick on to a floured board then cut the strips into diamond shapes and prick them with a fork.

5. Heat plenty on oil in a skillet and fry the fritters a few at a time.

6. Remove from the skillet when crisp and golden, drain on kitchen towels, and serve.
These fritters are also delicious served in syrup: Dissolve 1$^{1}/_{2}$ cups sugar in 2$^{1}/_{2}$ cups water brought to a boil. When reduced and thickened, remove from the heat, dip the fritters in the syrup, and serve warm or cold.

Chicken curry

Preparation: 1 hour 30 minutes

1 oven-ready chicken weighing $2^3/_4$ lb • $^1/_2$ cup ghee (see p. 9) • 1 onion, finely chopped • 2 cloves garlic, finely chopped • 1 tbsp ground coriander • 1 tbsp turmeric • 1 tbsp grated root ginger • $^1/_2$ tsp chili powder • $1^1/_2$ tbsp garam masala (see p. 10) • salt • $^2/_3$ cup water • $^2/_3$ cup natural yoghurt

1. Joint the chicken into 8 pieces. Remove and discard the skin.

2. Using a heavy-based saucepan or skillet, brown the chicken pieces evenly all over at a high temperature in about two thirds of the ghee to seal the meat. Remove from the saucepan and set aside.

3. Lightly sauté the finely chopped onion and garlic in the remaining ghee. Mix together the coriander, turmeric, ginger, chili powder, and garam masala, and add to the saucepan. After a minute or two put in the chicken and sprinkle with a little salt.

4. Mix the water with the yoghurt, pour over the chicken, and stir thoroughly. Lower the heat, cover, and cook slowly for 45–60 minutes, until the chicken is tender and comes easily off the bone. The sauce should be fairly liquid; if too liquid, however, thicken by raising the heat and cooking for a few minutes with the lid off. Serve hot.

Tandoori murghi (tandoori-baked chicken)

Preparation: 1 hour 10 minutes + 8 hours marinating time

1 chicken weighing 2³/₄ lb jointed into 8 pieces • 1 lemon • 1 tsp freshly ground black pepper • 1 onion, chopped • 2 cloves garlic • 1 tsp grated root ginger (or powdered ginger) • 1 tsp paprika • 2 tsp garam masala • 2 tsp ground coriander • 1 tsp ground cumin • 1 tsp chili powder • ¹/₂ tsp red food coloring (optional) • 1 cup natural yoghurt • 1 tbsp wine vinegar • 3 tbsp ghee (see p. 9)

1. Rinse and dry the chicken pieces. Remove the skin and, using a sharp knife, make oblique incisions in the fleshiest parts.

2. Rub over each chicken piece with a lemon, cut in half, rubbing it well into the crevices and incisions. Sprinkle with salt and pepper.

3. Blend the onion, garlic, and ginger in a food processor. Add and blend all the other spices and the food coloring if used. Lastly add the yoghurt and ginger and blend again to a smooth and creamy consistency.

4. Put the chicken into a deep dish and cover with the yoghurt sauce ensuring that each piece is completely covered by the sauce.

5. Cover with foil and marinate in the refrigerator for 8 hours or overnight. Turn the chicken pieces with a spoon occasionally to make sure that they are properly impregnated with the marinade.

6. Grease an ovenproof dish with the ghee. Transfer the coated chicken pieces to the dish and cover it with foil before cooking. In the absence of a traditional Indian *tandur*, cook in a very hot domestic oven heated to about 480°F.

7. Cook until tender, basting the chicken now and again with the marinating liquid. Serve with lettuce, onion, and lemon wedges.

Kashmiri red stewed lamb

Preparation: 1 hour 40 minutes

6 tbsp oil • 1³/₄-in piece cinnamon • 3 cloves • pinch ground asafoetida • 4 tsp paprika • 2¹/₄ lb boned lamb shoulder, cut into cubes • 3 cups natural yoghurt • 1 tsp ground ginger • 1 tsp ground fennel seeds • ¹/₂ tsp garam masala (see p. 10) • salt

1. Heat the oil in a large skillet or casserole and fry the spices until their aroma is released, adding one a few seconds after the other, in the following order: cinnamon, cloves, asafoetida, paprika.

2. Add the lamb cubes, stir, and brown all over in the spicy oil, then add the lightly beaten yoghurt. Mix together and add the ginger and the ground fennel seeds.

3. Stir everything again then pour in about 2¹/₄ cups hot water, cover, and simmer gently until the meat is tender.

4. A few minutes before the meat is done, add the garam masala, if necessary diluted in a little hot water to adjust the consistency of the gravy, and a little salt. Serve the stew hot with either plain boiled rice (chawal), chapatis (see p. 94) or naan (see p. 95).

Curried lamb

Preparation: 1 hour 40 minutes

1½–1¾ lb boned lamb shoulder ● 1 onion ● 2 cloves garlic ● ¼ cup ghee (see p. 9) ● 1 tsp chili powder ● 2 tsp freshly ground pepper ● 2 tsp ground coriander ● 1 tsp ground cumin ● 1 tsp ground turmeric ● 3 small, ripe tomatoes ● 1 lemon ● 1¼ cups thin meat broth ● 2 tsp garam masala (see p. 10) ● salt

1. Remove any fatty parts of the lamb. Cut the meat into 1-in cubes. Peel and thinly slice the onion and garlic.

2. Heat the ghee in a large saucepan and lightly fry the garlic and onion. Add, one at a time, the chili, pepper, coriander, cumin, and turmeric. Mix thoroughly.

3. Cut the tomatoes into quarters, place in the saucepan and stew until quite soft. Add the meat then sprinkle with lemon juice and little salt.

4. Pour in the hot broth and simmer softly for about 1 hour, stirring from time to time.

5. Stir in the garam masala last, check the seasoning, and simmer for a further 10 minutes. Ensure that the meat is tender before removing the saucepan from the heat.

6. Arrange the lamb pieces on a serving dish, pour over the hot sauce, and serve immediately.

Fish with vegetables

Preparation: 1 hour

1 whole fish (e.g. bass, bream, silver mullet etc.) weighing 2¼ lb • 1 eggplant • 1 zucchini • 1 potato • 1 tbsp salt • 1 tbsp turmeric • 1 fresh green chili pepper • 1 large tomato • 1 small piece root ginger • oil • ½ tsp Indian five-spice powder • ½ tsp sugar • 2 chopped dried chili peppers • ½ tsp ground coriander • ¼ tsp ground cumin • ¼ tsp garam masala (see p. 10) • 1 tbsp mustard seeds

1. Scale and clean the fish. Cut into 1$\frac{1}{2}$-in steaks.

2. Clean the eggplant and zucchini and peel the potato. Cut them into cubes. Mix the salt with the turmeric and sprinkle equally over the fish steaks and the vegetable cubes.

3. Trim and chop the fresh green chili pepper; chop the blanched, peeled and seeded tomato and grate the ginger.

4. Heat 2 tbsp oil in a flameproof casserole. Brown the fish, remove, and drain. Lightly fry the potato, remove and drain. Repeat the process with the eggplant and then the zucchini, adding more oil if necessary.

5. Fry the five-spice powder and the fresh chili in the same oil until they release their aroma then return the fish, potato, eggplant and zucchini to the casserole and add the tomato, the ginger, the sugar, and the remaining spices except for the mustard seeds.

6. Cover and cook over high heat, in just enough hot water to cover the ingredients.

7. Meanwhile pound the mustard seeds and mix with a little oil.

8. When the fish and greens are nearly done, add the mustard seeds and cook for no more than 5 minutes. Serve with plain boiled rice.

Braised fish with coconut milk

Preparation: 40 minutes

2 black peppercorns • 1 tsp mustard seeds • 1 tsp ground fenugreek • 1³/₄-in piece cinnamon • 1 tsp turmeric • 2 cloves • 2 dried chili peppers • 2 cloves garlic • 1¹/₄-in piece root ginger • 1 tsp garam masala (see p. 10) • fresh lemon juice • 1¹/₂ lb white fish fillets (e.g. sole or similar) • ¹/₄ cup ghee (see p. 9) • 1 onion • 1³/₄ cups coconut milk • salt • 1 tbsp chopped coriander leaves

1. Pulverize the first 10 ingredients in an electric grinder. Place the powder in a bowl and moisten with enough lemon juice to form a runny paste.

2. Spread this paste all over the fish fillets.

3. Heat the ghee in a nonstick saucepan. Fry the chopped onion and when it is a golden brown, add the fish fillets and gently fry on both sides.

4. Pour in the coconut milk, season with salt, cover and simmer slowly for about 15 minutes. Check the seasoning, transfer to a serving dish and sprinkle with the chopped coriander leaves.

Fish curry

Preparation: 45 minutes

1³/₄ lb fish fillets (e.g. cod, mackerel) • 1 onion • 1 clove garlic • ¹/₂ cup ghee (see p. 9) • 1 tsp ground fenugreek • 1 tsp ground coriander • 1 tsp ground cumin • 1 tsp freshly ground pepper • 1 tsp chili powder • 2 bay leaves • 2 tbsp tomato purée • 1¹/₄ cups boiling water • 1 lemon • salt

1. Cut the fish fillets into fairly large slices. Peel and chop the onion and garlic. Heat the ghee in a heavy casserole and brown the onion and garlic. Stir in all the spices and cook for 2–3 minutes.

2. Add the tomato purée, stir, and pour in the boiling water. Add the fish slices to the cooking liquid.

3. Bring to a boil, lower the heat, and simmer for 15 minutes.

4. Remove from the heat. Season and sprinkle with lemon juice before serving.

Shrimp with Jerusalem artichokes

Preparation: 40 minutes

10½ oz fresh or frozen large shrimp • 2 medium-sized potatoes • 2 lb Jerusalem artichokes • 2 onions • 2 fresh green chili peppers • 1½-in piece root ginger (optional) • 1 level tsp salt • 1 tsp turmeric • 2 tbsp oil

1. Peel the shrimp but leave the heads on. Peel and dice the potatoes and Jerusalem artichokes. Peel and chop the onions. Trim the chili peppers, remove the seeds and pith. Peel and grate the ginger (if used).

2. Mix the salt with the turmeric and, using your hands, mix the shrimp with the mixture, ensuring they are evenly coated.

3. Heat the oil in a deep skillet. Fry the onion, add the potato and chili and then the ginger. When these have cooked for a few minutes, add the Jerusalem artichokes and mix well.

4. Lastly, mix in the shrimp with a little hot water and cook, covered, for another 10 minutes. Serve this dish hot, preferably with plain boiled or pilau rice.

Parsee scrambled eggs

Preparation: 20 minutes

1 large, ripe tomato • ¼ cup ghee (see p. 9) • 1 small onion, chopped • 1 tsp grated root ginger • ½ tsp fresh, green chili pepper, seeded and chopped • ½ tsp ground turmeric • 8 eggs • 1 tbsp chopped coriander leaves • salt
½ tsp freshly ground pepper

1. Blanch and peel the tomato, remove the seeds, and chop coarsely.

2. Heat the ghee in a nonstick saucepan and fry the onion. Stir in the ginger, add the chili, the tomato, and the turmeric. Mix well.

3. Lightly beat the eggs with the chopped coriander, salt, and pepper.

4. Pour into the saucepan and scramble with a fork until the egg is the desired consistency.

Vegetable curry

Preparation: 1 hour 10 minutes

$3^{1}/_{2}$ oz carrots • 2 green bell peppers • $3^{1}/_{2}$ oz zucchini • $3^{1}/_{2}$ oz eggplant • $3^{1}/_{2}$ oz French beans • $3^{1}/_{2}$ oz freshly grated or desiccated coconut • 2 cloves garlic • 1 onion • $^{1}/_{4}$ cup ghee (see p. 9) • 1 tbsp grated root ginger • 1 tsp mustard seeds • 1 tsp freshly ground black pepper • 1 tsp ground cumin • 1 tsp ground coriander • 2 tsp turmeric • salt • 3 fresh green chili peppers • 3 tsp garam masala (see p. 10)

1. Wash and trim all the vegetables. Cut the carrots and peppers into $1^{1}/_{2}$-in matchsticks. Slice the zucchini and the eggplant. Cut the beans to the same length as the carrots and peppers. Place each prepared vegetable into a bowl of cold water until they are all ready.

2. Put the coconut into a liquidizer; bring $1^{1}/_{4}$ cups water to a boil and pour over the coconut. Liquidize until smooth.

3. Fry the peeled and finely chopped garlic and onion in a heavy-based casserole with the ghee; when they begin to color, add the ginger followed after a minute or two by the mustard, pepper, cumin, coriander, and turmeric. Mix well.

4. Drain and dry the vegetables. Add to the spices in sequence, starting with those which take longest to cook. Mix thoroughly. When the vegetables have absorbed the flavors, add the puréed coconut and a little salt, and bring to a boil.

5. Cover and simmer for 15 minutes, adding more hot water if needed. Meanwhile trim, seed, and finely slice the chilis.

6. Dissolve the garam masala in a little water and add to the casserole with the chilis. Cook for a further 5 minutes and serve piping hot.

Cachumber (Indian salad)

Preparation: 10 minutes

8 oz tomatoes • 2 oz onions • 1 lemon • 1 fresh green chili pepper • 2 tbsp chopped coriander leaves • salt • $^{1}/_{2}$ tsp freshly ground pepper

1. Slice the tomatoes and the onions. Place in a salad bowl and sprinkle with lemon juice.

2. Add the trimmed, seeded, and chopped chili pepper together with the chopped coriander. Season with salt and pepper, mix well, and serve.

Spiced rice with mint and coriander

Preparation: 30 minutes

1 cup basmati rice • ½ tsp saffron strands • 1 1¼-in piece cinnamon • 4 cloves • ¼ cup ghee (see p. 9) • 1 1¼-in piece root ginger • 1 onion • 1¼ cups natural yoghurt • 2 tbsp finely chopped coriander leaves • 2 tbsp finely chopped mint • salt • black pepper

1. Wash the rice well, place in a heavy-based saucepan, only just cover with cold water and bring to a boil.

2. Add the saffron, cook over medium heat for about 10 minutes, then drain.

3. Grind the cinnamon and cloves in a mortar. Preheat the ghee in a separate saucepan, add the cinnamon and cloves to it, and stir for about 1 minute.

4. Peel and finely chop the ginger and the onion. Add to the spices, stir, and fry.

5. Add the rice and mix thoroughly with the condiment juices.

6. Pour the yoghurt over the rice, add the coriander, mint, salt, and pepper. Reduce the heat and cook gently until the dish is warmed through.

Vegetable pilau

Preparation: 45 minutes

1 large onion • 2 cloves garlic • 5 oz carrots • 5 oz French beans • 5 oz potatoes • 5 oz turnips • ¼ cup ghee (see p. 9) • 1 tsp garam masala (see p. 10) • 1 tsp chili powder •

1 tsp turmeric • ½ tsp freshly ground black pepper
For the pilau rice: 1 cup basmati rice • 1 onion • ½ cup ghee (see p. 9) • 4 green and 2 black cardamoms • 6 cloves • 1 1-in piece cinnamon • 6 black peppercorns • 1 tsp cumin seeds (optional) • 2¼ cups water

1. Prepare the pilau rice. Wash the rice in lukewarm water. Drain well. Peel and finely chop the onion. Heat the ghee in a saucepan and fry the onion. Add the spices and cook for 1 minute.

2. Add the rice and stir in the spiced oil and onion mixture for 2 minutes or until the grains have absorbed the ghee and turned translucent. Meanwhile bring the water to a boil in a separate saucepan.

3. Pour the boiled water onto the rice and stir. Bring back to a boil, lower the heat and cover, leaving the lid very slightly ajar. Cook without stirring for 10–15 minutes at a gently simmer until the rice has absorbed the water. If more cooking is needed, add a few extra tablespoons of boiling water.

4. Prepare the vegetables. Peel the onion and cut into thin rings. Peel and cut the garlic into razor-thin slices. Scrape the carrots, cut lengthways into 4 strips, then cut each strip into ½-in slices. Trim and cut the beans into small pieces. Peel the potatoes and the turnip; cut into ¾-in cubes.

5. Fry the onion and the garlic in a saucepan with the ghee. Stir in the spices. Add the carrot, the potatoes, and the turnip and fry again.

6. Pour 1 cup salted hot water into the saucepan. Cook for about 10 minutes, add the beans and the peas, and finish cooking. When ready, the vegetables should be tender but not overdone, and the liquid reduced to a gravy in the bottom of the saucepan. Mix half of the vegetables with the rice. Lay the other half on top as decoration.

114

Rice with mango

Preparation: 30 minutes

1¼ cups basmati rice • salt • 1 firm mango • 4 cloves • 4 green cardamoms • ½ cup ghee (see p. 9) • 1 tsp turmeric • 1 tsp chili powder • 2 fresh red chili peppers

1. Wash the rice under running water. Cook in boiling salted water and drain just before the grains are cooked through.

2. Meanwhile peel the mango and cut in ½-in slices. Grind the cloves and the cardamoms to a powder in a mortar.

3. Heat the ghee in a large skillet. Stir in the turmeric, ground clove and cardamom powder, and chili powder and fry for 2 minutes.

4. Reduce the heat. Add the mango and cook until soft, turning the slices gently so that they do not break. Trim, remove the seeds and pith of the chilis and finely chop them.

5. Put the rice and the mango, together with the skillet juices, into a large serving bowl. Mix thoroughly, sprinkle with the chili, and serve.

Chilled yoghurt soup with mint

Preparation: 10 minutes

2¼ cups natural yoghurt • 1 cup light cream • 1¼ cups cold clear chicken broth • ½ tsp roasted cumin seeds • 2 tsp lemon juice • 2 tbsp finely chopped fresh mint • freshly ground black pepper • salt

1. Put the yoghurt in a bowl, add the cream, and lightly beat.

2. Pour in the broth a little at a time and stir until it is fully amalgamated.

3. Add the cumin seeds, the lemon juice, the mint, a pinch of ground black pepper, and salt to taste. Serve chilled.

Mulligatawny soup

Preparation: 1 hour

3 tbsp oil • 1 onion, chopped • 3 cloves garlic, chopped • 1 tsp grated root ginger • 14 oz stewing beef, diced • 2 carrots, diced • $^1/_2$ tsp turmeric • 1 tsp ground cumin • 1 tsp ground coriander • $^1/_2$ tsp ground fenugreek • $^1/_2$ tsp chili powder • 1 bay leaf • 3 black peppercorns • 4$^1/_2$ cups beef broth • 2 tbsp shredded coconut • 1 tbsp lemon juice • salt

1. Heat the oil in a heavy-based casserole. Fry the onion, garlic, and ginger.

2. Add the diced beef and carrot and fry gently for 2 minutes. Stir in all the spices and let their aroma develop.

3. Pour in the broth, bring to a boil, lower the heat, and simmer slowly until the ingredients are cooked through.

4. When nearly done, add the coconut, sprinkle with lemon juice, and test the seasoning. Serve hot as a main dish. Mulligatawny can be made with chicken and lentils instead of beef.

Jalebi (spiral fritters)

Preparation: 40 minutes + 3 hours standing time

2$\frac{1}{4}$ cups all-purpose flour • $\frac{2}{3}$ cup natural yoghurt • $\frac{1}{2}$ tsp saffron strands • 1 tsp dried yeast • 2$\frac{1}{2}$ cups sugar • 2$\frac{1}{4}$ cups water • 4 cloves • 4 green cardamoms • 1 stick cinnamon • $\frac{1}{4}$ cup rose water • oil for frying

1. Sieve the flour into a bowl and stir in the yoghurt.

2. Put the saffron in a cup. Fill three-quarters full with boiling water. When the water has cooled and turned color, stir in the yeast and 2 tsp sugar.

3. Pour through a strainer into the flour and yoghurt and mix into a smooth, fairly stiff batter adding a little extra water if necessary. Leave to stand at room temperature for 3 hours.

4. Meanwhile, prepare a syrup of $2\frac{1}{4}$ cups warmed water mixed with the remaining sugar, the cloves, the cardamoms, and the cinnamon. Leave to boil, stirring now and then, until the liquid has reduced to a thick syrup.

5. Remove from the heat, add the rose water then strain through a wide-meshed sieve.

6. When the batter is ready, heat plenty of oil in a deep-fryer to 370°F. Place the batter into a pastry bag fitted with a plain tube 1-in in diameter. Pipe batter spirals directly in the oil.

7. Fry the spirals until a deep gold all over. Remove and drain on kitchen towels.

8. Dip the spirals in the syrup and eat immediately while hot or serve cold. Jalebis are very popular in India as a snack sold on the streets.

Kulfi (Indian ice cream)

Preparation: 1 hour 30 minutes

9 cups milk • 10 green cardamoms • 5 tbsp sugar • 2 tbsp pistachio nuts, peeled and finely chopped • green food coloring (optional)

1. Pour the milk into a heavy-based saucepan, bring to a boil, lower the heat, add the cardamoms, and simmer until the milk has reduced to a third of its original volume, stirring frequently.

2. Remove and discard the cardamoms.

3. Add the sugar, the pistachios and, if used, the green food coloring; dissolve thoroughly, then transfer the mixture to another container to cool completely.

4. Process the mixture in an ice-cream maker, or place in a shallow freezer tray, and freeze, stirring every 15 minutes with a whisk to keep the mixture smooth. When fully frozen and amalgamated, the ice cream is ready. To serve it Indian style, fill conical molds with the ice cream mixture when still malleable. Freeze, unmold, and arrange the cones radially as illustrated, with glacé fruit and ice cream wafers.

Southeast Asia

The lands of Southeast Asia are rich in fruit. Here grows the mangosteen, once sought in vain by Queen Victoria who is said to have offered a reward for the chance to taste this exotic fruit. Papaya, ramboutan, pineapple, bananas, oranges, lemons, and coconut are, with the mangosteen, part of the inexhaustible natural bounty of countries like Indonesia and Thailand. Near Bangkok, in the markets of Damnoen Suduak, dexterous young women carve the fruits with little knives in sculptural displays of exotic shape and dazzling color. Such images emphasize the sunny nature of the people in this land of "rice and smiles." The metaphor is apt, for Thailand is the world's sixth largest producer of rice. The Thais say "come and eat my rice" when inviting you to a meal. Wherever you eat, a bowl of rice is set before you. The Indonesians serve rice steamed or fried or mixed with fish or meat. The Vietnamese flavor theirs with *nuoc mam*, a strong fish ketchup rich in amino acids, salts, and phosphorus which compensates for the low nutritional value of the rice. Other countries in Southeast Asia also eat fish and rice as a main diet, the fish often cut into small nuggets and similarly flavored with hot condiments, like the Thai *nam pla*, made of dried shrimp pounded with lemon juice, sugar, garlic, and plenty of hot green chili peppers. The favorite meats are poultry, beef and pork, cooked in curry or sweet and sour sauce or combined with rice, crabmeat or fried shrimp.

Stuffed crab (Thailand)

Preparation: 1 hour

4 cooked spider crabs (approximately 7 oz crabmeat) • ¼ cup ground lean pork • 3 cloves garlic, finely chopped • 1 scallion, finely chopped • 1 tsp freshly ground black pepper • 1 tsp fish essence (*nam pla*) • 1 egg • salt (optional) • 1 red chili pepper (or 2 small ones) • 1 tbsp chopped parsley • oil for frying

1. Pull off the legs of the crabs, prise open the body, and scoop out the flesh. Save the shells and discard the rest.

2. Chop the flesh and amalgamate with the pork, garlic, scallion, pepper, fish essence, and egg. Taste and add a little salt if necessary (the fish essence is very salty).

3. Spoon the mixture into the crab shells, gently packing it down.

4. Trim the hot chili pepper, remove the seeds and pith, and cut into small even strips. Sprinkle to taste over the mixture and add the parsley.

5. Place the stuffed shells in a bamboo or metal steamer, cover tightly and cook for 20 minutes, keeping the container clear of the boiling water. Remove from the heat.

6. Leave until the shells have cooled then deep-fry until the top of the filling is a golden brown. Eat hot or lukewarm as a first course.

Spicy scampi (Indonesia)

Preparation: 40 minutes

1 tbsp oil • 2 tbsp finely chopped onion • 1 clove garlic, crushed or finely chopped • 2 tsp chili sauce (see p. 10) • 1 tsp ground galangal or ginger • 1¾ cups peeled saltwater crayfish (scampi) • 2 tsp tamarind water • 1 tsp sugar • 1 bay leaf • 1 lemon balm leaf • 1 small bunch chives • ½ cup creamed coconut • salt to taste

1. Heat the oil in a heavy-based saucepan and brown the onion and garlic. When they begin to soften, add the chili sauce (*sambal ulek*) and the galangal, stir and cook for 1 minute.

2. Add the scampi, the tamarind water, and the sugar.

3. When the scampi have absorbed the liquid flavors, add the bay and lemon balm leaves and the chopped chives. Pour on the creamed coconut.

4. Thicken over low heat until the sauce has almost completely reduced. Add salt if necessary, remove from the heat, and serve.

Shrimp beignets

Preparation: 1 hour

7 oz giant shrimp tails • 2¹/₂ cups vegetable oil • 2 shallots • 1 leek • 1 clove garlic • ³/₄ cup all-purpose flour • ¹/₂ tsp salt • 2 eggs • pinch chili powder

1. Peel the shrimp. Cut each into 4–5 pieces and fry in a little hot oil for just under 5 minutes. Set aside.

2. Clean the saucepan. Heat a little more oil, slice the shallots, and fry for 3 minutes. Add the thinly sliced leek and chopped garlic. Cook gently for another 3–4 minutes.

3. Place the flour and salt in a bowl and hollow the middle. Break in the eggs and work them in the flour to make a batter. Add a little water if necessary but take care that the batter is not too runny.

4. Put the shrimp and vegetables in the batter, add the chili powder, and stir thoroughly.

5. Heat the remaining oil in a deep-fryer. Spoon nut-sized quantities of the batter mixture into the oil a few at a time and deep-fry until crisp and golden.

Chicken in white sauce (Indonesia)

Preparation: 1 hour 10 minutes + 1/2 hour marinating time

1 3-lb oven-ready chicken • 2 cloves garlic, minced or finely chopped • 1 tsp grated root ginger • 1 tsp ground coriander • 1/2 tsp ground cumin • 1 tsp fennel seeds • 1/2 tsp freshly ground black pepper • 1 clove, finely chopped • pinch grated nutmeg • 3 tbsp peanut oil • 1 onion, finely chopped • 1 1/4 cups chicken broth • 2 oz creamed coconut • salt • 1 small bunch chives • 1/2 lemon

1. Joint the chicken into 8 pieces. Mix together the garlic, ginger, coriander, cumin, fennel seeds, pepper, clove, and nutmeg.

2. Rub the mixture all over the chicken pieces and leave to marinate for 1/2 hour.

3. Heat the oil in a large skillet, lightly brown the onion, then brown the chicken pieces.

4. Pour in the preheated broth, the coconut, and a little salt. Bring to a boil, lower the heat, and cook until the chicken is tender.

5. A few minutes before the chicken is ready, add the chopped chives. Sprinkle with lemon juice just before serving and accompany the dish with boiled rice.

Braised chicken with noodles (Burma)

Preparation: 1 hour 15 minutes

1 3½-lb oven-ready chicken • salt • 1 tsp ground turmeric • 2 onions • 6 cloves garlic • 1 small piece root ginger (or 1 tsp ground ginger) • peanut oil • 2 tsp chili powder • 2 tbsp chick pea flour • 2 tbsp lentil flour • 1 cup coconut milk • 4 small leeks • 2 lemons • 3 hard-boiled eggs • 9 oz egg noodles

1. Joint the chicken into 8 pieces. Rub the salt and turmeric into each chicken piece. Place the pieces in a deep pot, with enough water to cover, bring to a boil, and simmer gently for 20 minutes or until the chicken is almost cooked.

2. Finely chop 1 onion, 2 cloves garlic, and the ginger. Take the chicken from the pot, remove the skin and bones, and cut in cubes. Save the cooking liquid.

3. Heat 2 tbsp oil in a large casserole and brown the prepared onion, garlic, ginger, and chili powder for 5 minutes. Add the chicken, stirring the pieces in the spicy flavors for few minutes.

4. Strain the reserved cooking liquid and add a sufficient quantity to the combined vegetable flours to mix into a smooth, runny batter. Pour on to the chicken pieces and stir thoroughly.

5. Bring to a boil, lower the heat, and add the coconut milk. Simmer, stirring frequently, until the liquid becomes thick and creamy, if necessary adding more water or flour to reach the right consistency. Season with salt, set aside and keep warm.

6. Prepare the accompaniments. Cut the remaining onion into thin rings and the lemons into segments, slice the leeks, quarter the eggs; arrange on small serving plates.

7. Boil the noodles in plenty of salted water. Drain completely and fry in very hot oil so that they turn crisp and golden. Dry on kitchen towels then place in a large serving bowl.

8. Slice the remaining garlic cloves and brown in the same oil. Serve the hot chicken and noodles with the egg and raw vegetable and garnish with the fried garlic.

127

Pork and chicken ragout (Philippines)

9 oz boned chicken breasts • 1 lb lean pork • 1 clove garlic • 1 onion • 2 bay leaves • 1 tbsp dark soy sauce • ½ cup white wine vinegar • salt • pepper • 1 tbsp chopped bacon fat

Preparation: 1 hour 15 minutes + 30 minutes marinating time

1. Cut the chicken and the pork into large pieces. Place in a bowl.

2. Add the finely chopped garlic and onion, the bay leaves, the soy sauce, and the vinegar. Sprinkle on salt and pepper. Stir and turn the ingredients so that the meat absorbs the flavors. Marinate for ½ hour.

3. Transfer the contents of the bowl to a saucepan, cover with cold water, and bring to a boil. Lower the heat and simmer for about 1 hour until the meats are tender and a little cooking liquid is left.

4. Pour the remaining liquid into a bowl. Set the meat aside.

5. Melt the bacon fat and fry the pieces of meat over high heat.

6. When browned on all sides, soak the meat with the reserved cooking liquid and simmer over low heat for about 5 minutes. Serve the ragout very hot accompanied by plain boiled rice.

Braised beef (Burma)

Preparation: 1 hour 20 minutes + 4 hours marinating time

1³/₄ lb braising beef • 1 tbsp fish essence (*nuoc mam*) • 1 tbsp white wine vinegar • ¹/₂ tsp ground turmeric • 2 chopped onions • 2 cloves garlic, chopped • 1 tbsp grated root ginger • 1 tsp chili powder • 4 tbsp peanut oil • 3 bay leaves • 1 1¹/₄-in piece cinnamon • 5 black peppercorns • 2 cloves • salt

1. Cut the meat into 1¹/₄-in cubes. Marinate for 4 hours in a mixture of the fish essence, vinegar, and turmeric, turning the meat occasionally.

2. After the marination, combine the onion, garlic, ginger, and chili and fry the mixture in a large saucepan with hot oil at a brisk temperature, stirring constantly, until the aromas are released.

3. When the onion is golden brown add the meat, bay leaves, cinnamon, peppercorns, and cloves.

4. Fill the saucepan with water just over halfway to the level of the meat. Add a little salt, cover, and simmer for about 1 hour or until the meat is fork-tender. If the liquid level gets too low, replace with a little preheated water.

5. When the dish is ready, remove the whole spices, test for seasoning, and serve hot.

Fried or broiled pork spareribs (Kampuchea)

Preparation: 40 minutes + 30 minutes marinating time

3 cloves garlic • 2¼ lb pork spareribs • 2 tbsp fish essence (*nuoc mam*) • ½ tbsp sugar • pinch freshly ground black pepper • 1 red chili pepper • 1 small bunch parsley • 3 tbsp peanut oil

1. Peel the garlic and chop very finely.

2. Place the spareribs in a bowl and cover with the garlic, fish essence, sugar, and pepper. Turn the meat so that it absorbs the flavors and leave to marinate for 30 minutes.

3. Meanwhile wash and trim the chili, remove the seeds, and pith and cut into small strips. Wash and dry the parsley.

4. When the meat has finished marinating, heat the oil in a skillet or wok and fry the spareribs until they are golden brown and crisp on all sides.

5. Remove the spareribs from the skillet, drain them thoroughly and arrange on a serving dish. Decorate with the chili strips and small sprigs of parsley. Serve hot, accompanied by plain or savory rice.

If preferred, the spareribs can be broiled or barbecued after marinating, instead of being fried.

Beef Sumatra (Indonesia)

Preparation: 3 hours 40 minutes

1³/₄ lb braising beef • 1 tsp coriander seeds • ¹/₂ tsp cumin seeds • ¹/₂ tsp fennel seeds • ¹/₂ tsp black peppercorns • 1 tsp ground turmeric • 1 large onion • 1 tsp grated root ginger • 2 cloves garlic • 6 red chilis, trimmed and seeded • ¹/₂ oz dried tamarind • ¹/₄ cup boiling water • 1 small bunch chives • 4¹/₂ cups coconut milk • salt • 1 tsp cane sugar

1. Cut the meat into 1-in cubes. Place the coriander, cumin, fennel, peppercorns, and turmeric in an electric grinder and pulverize. Add the chopped onion, ginger, garlic, and chilis and blend with the spices to a smooth paste.

2. Put the tamarind in a small bowl and cover with the boiling water. Wait at least 6–7 minutes, squash the tamarind with a fork, remove it, and squeeze the juice from the pulp into the bowl. Discard the tamarind and save the water.

3. Place the meat in a large saucepan with the spicy paste, tamarind water, finely chopped chives, and coconut milk. Add salt to taste. Bring to a boil and cook for 3 hours over low heat, stirring often, especially toward the end, to ensure the stew does not stick to the bottom.

4. Add the sugar a few minutes before the dish is done, stir thoroughly, and see whether extra salt is needed. The meat should be fork-tender and the gravy very thick. Serve hot or cold.

Thai fish stew (Thailand)

Preparation: 1 hour 15 minutes

1½ lb fish fillets • 2 shallots • 2 cloves garlic • 2 fresh red chili peppers • 2 fresh green chili peppers • ¼ cup sunflower oil • 2 tsp shrimp paste (*blachan*) • 4 oz French beans • 1 small cauliflower • 4 oz bamboo shoots • 10 button mushrooms • 1 tsp fish essence (*nam pla*) • pinch chili powder • salt • 1 sprig coriander

1. Broil the fish fillets lightly. Mash about 3½–4 oz with a fork and cut the remaining fish into pieces.

2. Coarsely chop the shallots. Chop the garlic very finely. Trim and seed the chili peppers and cut into tiny pieces. Sauté together in hot oil for 2 minutes.

3. Add the shrimp paste, cook for another 4 minutes, then add the mashed fish and mix to a smooth cream.

4. Cut the beans into small pieces. Divide the cauliflower into little florets. Wash and trim the bamboo shoots. Trim the mushrooms.

5. Boil 2¼ cups water in large saucepan. Stir in the fish cream, blending thoroughly. Remove the surface scum that forms and add all the prepared vegetables. When these are tender, add the fish essence, chili powder, and salt to taste.

6. Add the fish pieces and bring back to boiling point. Lower the heat and cook for a few minutes. Transfer to a serving dish and garnish with coriander leaves.

Escabeche (Philippines)

Preparation: 50 minutes

1 large green bell pepper • 1 onion • 3 cloves garlic • peanut oil • 1 tsp grated root ginger (or ½ tsp ground ginger) • 4 thick fish steaks (e.g. cod, hake or similar) • all-purpose flour • salt • 1 tbsp cornstarch • 3 tbsp white wine vinegar • 1 tbsp cane sugar

1. Wash the pepper, cut it into quarters, remove the seeds and pith, and cut into strips ¼ in wide. Peel the onion and slice into thin rings. Chop the peeled garlic.

2. Heat 1¼ tbsp oil and brown the garlic and the ginger, followed immediately by the onion, then the pepper. Stir, and cook for several minutes; remove the onion and pepper when tender and set aside.

3. Dust the fish with flour. Add extra oil to the same saucepan or skillet and fry the fish until golden and crisp. Drain on kitchen towels and lightly season with salt on both sides while still hot.

4. Mix the cornstarch with 3 tbsp warm water. Pour into a saucepan with 1 cup more warm water, the vinegar, sugar, and little salt. Bring to a boil then lower the heat to a simmer.

5. Stir well, put in the fish steaks, and cook gently while the sauce reduces.

6. When the sauce has sufficiently thickened, add the vegetables that had been set aside, stirring them gently into the sauce. Adjust the seasoning, remove from the heat, and place the fish on a serving dish. Cover with the sauce, arrange the vegetables around the fish, and serve piping hot.

Bali style fish fillets (Indonesia)

Preparation: 45 minutes

1 2-lb sea bass or similar fish • 1 tbsp grated root ginger • 3 cloves garlic, chopped • $^1/_2$ onion, chopped • 2 dried red chilis • $^1/_2$ oz dried tamarind • peanut oil • 1 tbsp soy sauce • 1 tbsp brown sugar • $^1/_2$ tsp salt

1. Clean and wash the fish; fillet and cut into strips. Put the ginger, garlic, onion, and chilis in an electric grinder and blend to a purée.

2. Soften the tamarind in a small cup of boiling water. When cool, remove the tamarind and rub the fish with it.

3. Heat 2 tbsp oil in a heavy saucepan. Fry the puréed ingredients for about 1 minute before adding the soy sauce, sugar, and salt. Mix with $^1/_4$ cup water, bring to a boil, and simmer over lowered heat for about 2 minutes. Set the sauce aside and keep warm.

4. Fry the fish fillets in a little hot oil for about 3–4 minutes. Dry on kitchen towels then lay the fillets on a serving dish and pour on the sauce before serving.

Fish parcels (Burma)

Preparation: 50 minutes

1½ lb thick fillets of white fish • 2 tsp salt • ½ tsp ground turmeric • 3 small onions • 2 cloves garlic • 1 tsp ground ginger • ½ tsp chili powder • 1 tbsp rice flour • ½ cup coconut milk • 1 tbsp oil • 3 chives, chopped • 12 Chinese cabbage leaves

1. Pat the fish fillets dry with kitchen towels. Cut into 2-in squares. Place on a stainless steel tray. Rub the fish pieces with half of the salt and turmeric.

2. Peel, chop, and purée the onion and garlic. Add the ginger, chili, rice flour, the remaining salt, and turmeric.

3. Incorporate the coconut milk, oil, and chives into the mixture, working them in with your hands.

4. Wash the Chinese leaves, drain well, and cut across the middle of the leaves. Spoon a little of the onion mixture on to the center of 12 of the leaf halves.

5. Cover the onion mixture with a fish fillet then another layer of the mixture and top with the other half leaf.

6. Overlap the bottom and top leaves and wrap together with twine or raffia. Cook in a steamer for 20 minutes. Serve the parcels immediately.

In Burma, banana leaves are usually used as wrappers.

Fried bananas (Indonesia)

Preparation: 30 minutes

4 firm bananas • $^1/_2$ cup rice flour • salt • 1 piece ghee (see p. 9) • $^2/_3$ cup coconut milk • oil for frying

1. Sieve the flour into a large bowl together with 2 pinches of salt. Add the ghee and the coconut milk. Beat vigorously with a balloon whisk until the ingredients have blended into a smooth batter.

2. Peel the bananas, cut them in half lengthways and immerse them in the batter.

3. Heat enough oil to cover the bottom of a large heavy-based skillet. Fry the bananas, leaving enough space between them to prevent them from sticking together.

4. Brown well on the underside, turn over, and brown until both sides are the same color.

Fried bananas go very well with meat dishes or heavily-spiced vegetables.

Piquant mixed vegetable stew (Indonesia)

Preparation: 40 minutes

1/2 oz dried tamarind • oil • 1 onion, chopped • 1 clove garlic, chopped • 2 fresh chili peppers, trimmed, seeded and chopped • 1/2 tsp ground ginger • 1/2 tsp shrimp paste • 2 1/4 lb mixed vegetables (e.g. cabbage, French beans, zucchini, carrots) • salt • 4 almonds, peeled and chopped

1. Soften the tamarind in a small bowl of boiling water. When softened, remove and squeeze its juice into the cooled water. Reserve the water.

2. Heat the oil and brown the onion and garlic, stirring. After 2 minutes add the chilis, ginger, and shrimp paste. Mix together.

3. Slice the vegetables and add to the mixture in stages, starting with those that take longest to cook. Add a little hot water and simmer gently.

4. After a few minutes, pour in the tamarind water. Add salt if necessary. Sprinkle with the chopped almonds before serving.

Thai salad (Thailand)

Preparation: 15 minutes

1 tbsp whole shelled peanuts • 1 heaping tbsp dried shrimp • 2 cloves garlic, finely chopped • 7 oz white cabbage, thinly sliced • 3 carrots, scraped and shredded • 2 tbsp lemon juice • 1 tbsp fish essence (*nam pla*) • pinch sugar • 2 tbsp sesame seed oil • salt • freshly ground black pepper

1. Warm a nonstick saucepan over gentle heat and roast the peanuts in it until they turn brown. Take the peanuts out of the saucepan, allow them to cool a little, then rub them between the palms of your hands to remove their skins.

2. When the peanuts have cooled down completely grind them to a powder in an electric grinder. Grind the dried shrimp.

3. Place all the ingredients, prepared as indicated, into a large salad bowl, mix them together, and season to taste with salt and freshly ground pepper.

Salad vegetables like cucumber, tomato, and lettuce can be prepared with the same dressing.

Tofu salad (Indonesia)

Preparation: 30 minutes

1 cucumber • salt • 9 oz tofu (bean curd) • oil for frying •
3¹/₂ oz bean sprouts • 3 tbsp peanut sauce (see p. 10)

1. Slice the cucumber thinly and sprinkle with salt. Cut the bean curd into cubes, fry on all sides in hot oil, and drain on kitchen towels.

2. Rinse the cucumber slices under running cold water, pat dry with a cloth, and arrange in layers on a serving dish with the fried bean curd cubes laid on top.

3. Put the bean sprouts into a bowl of cold water. Take the bean sprouts out of the water leaving behind any that have sunk to the bottom of the bowl. Cook the sprouts in boiling water for a short minute, remove, drain thoroughly, and lay over the cucumber and bean curd with the peanut sauce on top.

Sautéed rice with sausage

Preparation: 1 hour

salt • 1 cup basmati rice • 3 eggs • oil • 4 tbsp dried shrimp • 3 Chinese sausages • 1 onion • few slices cooked ham • 2 tbsp chopped shrimp • freshly ground black pepper

1. Boil plenty of salted water in a heavy enamelled saucepan. Wash the rice under running cold water until it runs clear, add to the saucepan, cook until tender, drain, and leave to cool.

2. With the beaten eggs fry an omelet in a little oil. Leave to cool. Cut in strips.

3. Soften the dried shrimp in warm water and mince the sausages.

4. Finely chop the onion and the ham.

5. Sauté the onion in a large saucepan with a little oil. Pour in the cooked rice and amalgamate with the oil to separate the grains.

6. Add the omelet strips, the chopped shrimp, the drained dried shrimp, sausage, and the ham. Mix together. Season with salt and pepper to taste and mix again.

Serve as a main course or as part of a selection of dishes.

Coconut-flavored rice (Indonesia)

1 cup long-grain rice • 2¼ cups coconut milk (*santen*) • 3 curry leaves • 1 chive • 2 bay leaves • salt

Preparation: 30 minutes

1. Wash the rice in a large sieve until the water runs clear. Drain well.

2. Pour the coconut milk into a large saucepan. Add the rest of the ingredients with the rice, stir, and bring to a boil.

3. Lower the heat to minimum, cover, and cook until the coconut milk has been completely absorbed and the rice is tender but still firm: the time will depend on the quality of the rice (if necessary, add a little hot water).

4. Serve decorated with strips of omelet, fried onion rings, and cucumber slices.

144

Noodles with mixed vegetables and meat (Philippines)

Preparation: 1 hour

7 oz thin egg noodles • ¹/₂ cup oil • 1 clove garlic, chopped • 7 oz lean pork, finely diced • 7 oz finely diced chicken breast • 1 cup shrimp, chopped • 1 onion, chopped • 3¹/₂ oz cabbage, shredded • ¹/₂ cup chicken broth • 2 tbsp fish essence (*patis*) • pinch chili powder • pinch freshly ground black pepper • salt • 2 hard-boiled eggs • 1 lemon in segments • 2 scallions, sliced

1. Cook the noodles, place in a sieve under running cold water and drain well. Transfer to a bowl and mix with 1 tbsp oil to prevent them from sticking together.

2. Heat 1 tbsp oil in a large skillet or, preferably, a wok. Fry the noodles until they are golden, dry on kitchen towels, and set aside on a plate.

3. Wipe the skillet clean and sauté the garlic in 1 tbsp oil. Add the diced pork and stir until it browns all over.

4. Add the diced chicken. When it has turned color raise the heat and add the shrimp. Stir-fry for few minutes, remove from the heat, and set aside.

5. Wipe the skillet again and heat more oil. Fry the onion until it softens. Add the cabbage and stir with a wooden spoon until it is cooked but still crisp.

6. At this stage pour in the chicken broth with the fish essence, chili powder and pepper and mix together. Add the meats and shrimp, stir, then add the noodles and salt to taste. Mix everything again and reheat before serving.

7. Place the noodles on a large serving plate and decorate with the eggs cut into quarters, lemon segments, and scallion rings.

Crispy rice noodles (Thailand)

Preparation: 40 minutes

2 tsp cane sugar • 1 tsp vinegar • oil for frying • 7 oz rice noodles • 2 tbsp peanut oil • 1 onion, finely chopped • 2 cloves garlic, finely chopped • $3^{1}/_{2}$ oz lean pork, cut into small cubes • 1 cup peeled shrimp • $^{1}/_{3}$ cup crabmeat • 2 tbsp soy sauce • salt • 2 sprigs coriander • grated rind of 1 orange • 2 cleaned fresh chili peppers, shredded

1. Dissolve the sugar in a little water acidulated with the vinegar. Stir.

2. Heat the frying oil in a large saucepan or skillet. Add the noodles a little at a time, brown until crisp, drain, and dry off the excess oil on kitchen towels.

3. Using a separate skillet or preferably a wok, heat the peanut oil and stir-fry the onion and garlic.

4. Add the pork and stir-fry to ensure even cooking.

5. Add the shrimp and the crabmeat and mix with the pork.

6. Pour in the soy sauce and dissolved sugar, add the fried noodles, season with a little salt, and mix thoroughly.

7. Remove the coriander stalks with scissors.

8. Pour the contents of the wok onto a serving plate and decorate with chopped coriander, grated orange rind, and strips of chili pepper. Serve hot.

Fried noodles (Indonesia)

Preparation: 20 minutes

9 oz egg noodles ● 3 tbsp oil ● ¹/₂ onion, finely chopped ● 2 cloves garlic, finely chopped ● 1 stick celery, chopped ● 5 oz chicken breasts or lean pork, finely diced ● ¹/₂ cup peeled shrimp, chopped ● 2 tbsp light soy sauce ● salt ● pepper

1. Cook the noodles in plenty of water leaving them slightly underdone. Drain.

2. Heat the oil in a large skillet. Sauté the onion, garlic, and celery. Add the chicken or pork and shrimp.

3. Mix together and cook over medium heat. Add the noodles, stir well, and sprinkle with the soy sauce, salt, and pepper.

4. Let the noodles absorb the flavors for a minute or so before serving very hot.

Duck soup with bamboo shoots (Vietnam)

1 tbsp dried bamboo shoots • 5 shallots • 1 3½-lb oven-ready duck • 1 tbsp salt • freshly ground black pepper • 1 tsp sugar • 4 tbsp *nuoc mam* sauce (or diluted anchovy paste) • 9 oz rice flour noodles • 2 small scallions • 3 sprigs coriander

Preparation: 2 hours + 2 hours soaking time including 1 hour marinating time

1. Soak the bamboo shoots in hot water for 2 hours then drain thoroughly. Skin the shallots and reduce to a purée in an electric blender. Sprinkle the duck with salt and pepper and cover with the shallot purée. Leave to marinate for 1 hour.

2. Bring 5½ cups water to a boil in a large saucepan. Add the whole duck and the bamboo shoots. Simmer for 15 minutes, skimming the surface continually.

3. Add the sugar and mix in with the *nuoc mam* sauce. Cover and finish the cooking over a low simmer for about 1 hour. The bamboo shoots should take on an elastic consistency.

4. Meanwhile, cook the rice flour noodles separately for 5 minutes in 9 cups boiling water. Drain and rinse quickly under running cold water.

5. Skin the scallions and cut into thin rings. Wash and dry the coriander and cut off the leaves with scissors.

6. Remove the duck from the saucepan and joint into 8 portions.

7. Put a portion of duck and noodles into each individual bowl, together with a few bamboo shoots, and cover with the duck broth.

8. Garnish the soup with the coriander leaves and scallion rings.

Fish soup with radish (Burma)

Preparation: 1 hour

9 oz white fish fillets • 1 tsp turmeric • salt • 1 tamarind (or 1 oz dried tamarind) • 1 tsp shrimp paste (*ngapi*) • 1 tbsp fish essence (*nuoc mam*) • 1 onion • 2 cloves garlic • 4 tomatoes • 1 sprig coriander • 2 tbsp oil • 1 tsp grated root ginger • 9 oz white radish

1. Dry the fish fillets with a clean cloth and cut them into pieces. Lay the pieces on a tray, dust with turmeric, and allow a few minutes for the seasoning to saturate.

2. Put the tamarind into a bowl, cover with hot water, and leave to infuse. Mix the shrimp paste with the *nuoc mam*. Chop the onion, garlic, and tomatoes. Chop the coriander leaves. Heat the oil in a large heavy-based saucepan. Sauté the garlic, onion, and ginger. Add the fish morsels, turning them delicately, and stir in the *nuoc mam* sauce and tomatoes.

3. Pour in 6¼ cups cold water, bring to a boil, lower the heat, and simmer for 15 minutes. Trim and slice the radish and add it to the simmering ingredients.

4. Remove the tamarind, squeeze its juice back into the bowl (if necessary, soak and squeeze the tamarind again), then pour the tamarind water into the saucepan.

5. Cook for a further 15 minutes. Just before serving, sprinkle the soup with chopped coriander leaves. Turn off the heat, leave to stand for a few minutes, uncovered, then serve.

Tapioca and crabmeat soup (Kampuchea)

Preparation: 35 minutes

½ cup tapioca • 4 shallots, finely chopped • 1 tbsp peanut oil • 1 cup crabmeat (fresh, canned or frozen) • 5½ cups chicken broth • 1 small tsp *nuoc mam* sauce or anchovy paste (optional) • 2 sprigs fresh coriander or chervil • 2 small scallions • salt and pepper

1. Soak the tapioca in water for about 10 minutes. Meanwhile, peel the shallots.

2. Heat the oil in a medium-sized saucepan or skillet and brown the shallots over gentle heat. Stir in the crabmeat, fry for a few minutes, then pour in the broth and the *nuoc mam* or anchovy paste.

3. Drain the tapioca, place in the saucepan, and bring to a boil. Lower the heat and simmer for 5 minutes, or until the tapioca is translucent.

4. Wash the coriander and cut the leaves into little pieces. Skin the scallions and slice into rounds.

5. When the tapioca has cooked, ladle it into 4 individual bowls. Add salt and pepper to taste, the coriander and scallions, and serve hot.

If using fresh crab, the water in which it is cooked provides a good substitute for the chicken broth.

Coconut-coated tapioca bouchées (Thailand)

1 cup tapioca • 1 cup cane sugar • ½ tsp salt • 3 cups water • 1 tbsp oil • 1 cup freshly grated or desiccated coconut • 2 tsp confectioner's sugar

Preparation: 30 minutes (+ 30–40 minutes cooling time)

1. Put the tapioca in a saucepan with the cane sugar and salt. Add the indicated amount of water little by little, stirring constantly.

2. Bring to a boil, lower the heat, and simmer for about 10 minutes, still stirring, until the mixture thickens and turns almost transparent.

3. Oil a shallow pan or mold with a pastry brush.

4. Pour the mixture into the mold and leave to cool completely.

5. Mix the coconut with the confectioner's sugar.

6. Spoon out nut-sized portions of the mixture and roll each portion in the sugared coconut. Arrange attractively on a bed of green leaves.

Toasted semolina diamonds (Burma)

Preparation: 2 hours 30 minutes

1 cup semolina • 1 cup cane sugar • ¹/₂ tsp salt • 1¹/₄ cups coconut milk (or diluted creamed coconut) • ¹/₂ cup butter • 3 eggs • ¹/₂ cup seedless white raisins, soaked in water • 4 tbsp sesame seeds

1. Place the semolina in a large nonstick saucepan. Toast over low heat for about 10 minutes, carefully stirring and turning until the grains are a browny gold color.

2. Boil 4¹/₂ cups water. Remove the saucepan of semolina from the heat, add the cane sugar, salt, coconut milk, and boiling water, stir well, and leave for 30 minutes to set a little.

3. Return the saucepan to the heat and cook for 15 minutes to reduce the contents further. Turn off the heat, add about three quarters of the butter, and mix with the ingredients until completely melted. Leave to cool a little.

4. Break the eggs into a bowl, beat with a fork and stir quickly into the mixture. Heat the oven to 400°F.

5. Return the saucepan to the heat again, add the seedless white raisins and simmer for a further 10 minutes, occasionally stirring. The mixture should be thick and sticky.

6. Oil a square cake pan with the remaining butter. Pour in the mixture, smooth over the surface with a spatula dipped in oil, and dust with the sesame seeds, patting them down with the spatula.

7. Bake for 1¹/₂ hours in the preheated oven or until the mixture comes away from the sides of the pan and the sesame seeds are a nice gold color.

8. When it has cooled, carefully unmold the mixture and cut into diamond shapes about ¹/₂ in thick.

154

Glossary

Oriental countries produce a rich variety of natural foods. Some of these foods are native to one region, others grow to a varying extent throughout the East while many others still are commonly found in both East and West. Improved communications and transport techniques have increased the exportability of these foods, which now appear regularly on Western tables and can be grown outside of their traditional environments. While adequate substitutes exist for products that may not be readily available, it is hoped that this glossary will benefit the less-informed reader who wishes to learn more about the ingredients and techniques that go into the preparation of authentic Oriental dishes.

Abalone. An edible mollusk with smooth, firm flesh, considered to be a delicacy by the Chinese. Abalone is sold in cans or in dried form, depending on type and quality. The canned variety is easier to prepare and once opened, will keep in the refrigerator, covered in water, which should be changed daily. Dried abalone will keep indefinitely, if stored in a dry place.

Aduki see **Soy**.

Agar-agar. A gelatinous solidifying agent for puddings, sweetmeats, and jellies, also used in commercial ice-cream making. Widely used in Malaysia, Burma, Japan, and China, agar-agar is obtained from certain seaweeds and retains a slight seaweed taste. It is sold in powdered form, or in layers, threads or strips. The solid varieties of agar-agar have to be dissolved in cold water for 30 minutes before use. Alternatively it can be softened in hot water and eaten as it is, in salads and appetizers. Gelatin and other setting agents or thickeners like cornstarch can be substituted if agar-agar is unavailable.

Asafoetida. A resinous gum extracted from the plant *Ferula foetida*, a shady perennial native to Iran and Afghanistan and grown in India, where asafoetida is known as *hing*. The product is available ground or in crystals from Indian shops or chemists. Asafoetida has a pungent garlic-like taste and is valued as a digestive aid. It is used sparingly to season various appetizers, vegetable and pulse dishes, and sauces.

Awamori. A Japanese aquavit distilled from rice, appreciated in the West for its delicate taste.

Bamboo shoots. The spontaneous germination of bamboo happens mainly during the wet season. In China and Japan the little shoots, called respectively *tung shuon* and *takenoko*, are eaten as a vegetable. Bamboo shoots are also available in cans, already cooked and preserved in water. Once out of the can, the shoots can be stored in the refrigerator for some time if kept immersed in water. The dried variety should be soaked overnight in warm water before use.

Bamboo steamer. A practical, Chinese basket-like utensil for steaming food over a wok. The woven, porous bamboo structure lets the steam out naturally, thus preventing any condensation from the lid dripping over the food. Bamboo steamers are available in several sizes, the smaller ones being suitable for cooking *chiao tzu* and *hsao mai* (steamed dumplings).

To use a steamer, first fill a wok two-thirds full of water; place the steamer on top and heat the water until a cloud of steam builds up, before putting the prepared ingredients into the steamer. From time to time add more hot water to the wok. Care must be taken to maintain the level and temperature of the water (if cold water is added the sudden drop in temperature will interrupt the flow of steam).

Another useful feature of the steamer is that several can be stacked one on top of the other, enabling a whole meal to be cooked simultaneously. Plain, or "dry" food, like *hsao mai*, is laid directly on the bamboo, while ingredients that are moist or fatty should be placed first on a heat-resistant plate (or a cabbage or lotus leaf). New bamboo primer "baskets" should be immersed for at least 10 minutes in gently boiling water before use.

Basmati rice. This Indian rice, with its small, pointed, slender grains and delicate flavor, goes particularly well with spiced dishes.

Bean curd (tofu) see **Soy bean curd**

Bean sprouts see **Soy**

Bento box. A lidded tin box with compartments, used in Japan for snacks or picnics.

Betel (leaves). In India, the edible leaf of the *Piper belle*, a relative of the pepper plant, is widely chewn for its digestive properties and as a mouth cleanser, in the manner of chewing gum. The small heart-shaped leaves are folded around different fillings and secured with a clove. Fillings vary from ordinary spices, areca-nut parings or choicer lemon or lemon peel paste mixtures to luxury confections of edible gold and silver leaf. These little leaf parcels are known as *pan* or *paan*. Some varieties will stain the mouth a deep red. *Pans* are often passed around at the end of elegant dinner parties, on valuable salvers or in precious boxes known as *paan daan*. Commercially prepared *pans* tend to be very elaborate but traditionally it has always been, and in the main still is, the woman of the house who makes the *pans*, spending time and care in their preparation. The chewing of spices in India as digestives or carminatives is also customary without the betel wrapper; in such cases, the spices are usually roasted first.

Black bean paste. Available from Oriental foodstores, this paste is used in a variety of Chinese dishes.

Black chick pea flour. This fine, yellowish flour, called *besan, baisen* or *ganthia*, is ground from black Indian chick peas and widely used for making bread and batters, or for thickening sauces. A nutritious produce rich in protein, the flour is best sifted before use.

Black salt. Indian *kalanamak* is an impure "black" mineral salt containing traces of extraneous minerals such as sulphur. This gives it a very distinctive taste. Used in parts of India to flavor salads and appetizers, black salt is hard to find in the West but is not in any case essential to Oriental cooking.

Bombay duck. This misleadingly-named product derives from a small herring-like fish called bummalo, probably taken from the Indian *bombil*, which thrives in the murky dock waters of the ports along the west coast of India. The fish is baked dry in the sun and salted. The dried product has a peculiarly strong smell. In India, Bombay duck is usually eaten broiled or fried as an appetizer or snack, or served cooked in various sauces as a side dish or main dish. It is available from specialist grocers in the West.

Bonito flakes see **Fish flakes, dried.**

Capsicum see **Chili pepper**

Caraway. An umbelliferous plant which grows wild in Europe and parts of Asia. The small green seeds have a pungent, sweetish taste, stronger than cumin, with which they are sometimes confused. Caraway seeds are used in bakery products as well as certain dishes. Strongly aromatic, they are available whole or in powdered form.

Cardamom. The fruit capsule of the cardamom plant, a herbaceous perennial native to India, is a versatile spice, rich in essential oils, used in many savory and sweet dishes either on its own or mixed with other spices. Known in India as *elaychi*, cardamom is one of the ingredients used in the preparation of *garam masala* (q.v., see also recipe on p. 10). The most notable varieties are the green cardamom, of which only the seed ($^1/_2$ in in diameter) is used, and the black cardamom, a larger species (about $1^1/_2$ in), is used whole, including the pod.

Cardamoms used for rice flavoring are boiled whole, while only the seeds ground and roasted, are used to flavor spiced dishes. In India, cardamoms are used to perfume tea or coffee. Whole or ground cardamom is widely available.

Cashew nuts. These are the kernels of the stone-fruit of an Indian mahogany variety. *Kaju*, or the cashew nut, is almond-like with a brown leathery shell and a sweet kernel. Often eaten raw, these nuts are particularly popular when roasted or salted.

Cayenne pepper see **Chili pepper**

Chili pepper. This very common small hot pepper is used as a condiment, fresh, dried or in powdered form. Chili is available in many varieties, shapes and colors. It is indispensable in Oriental cookery and widely adopted in the rest of the world. It should not be forgotten that the hottest parts of the common red and green varieties are the pith and the seeds, which are used for making the powdered version, and these should be removed before eating. Hot or medium-hot chilis are varieties of *capsicum annuum*, originating in the tropics and including some 30 known species. Among these are the *lalmirch* or *mirchi* of India; the green *lombok idiju*, the red *lombok merah* used for making *sambal ulek* (see recipe on p. 11) and the small, extra hot red or green *lombok rawit* of Indonesia and Malaysia, a variety used for pickling which has to be rinsed before use. Most chilis are used fresh, dried or in one of the powdered varieties, for example, cayenne pepper. The hot chili taste is the best known feature of a properly spiced Indian curry dish.

Chili sauce (Sambal ulek). An Indonesian sauce widely used as an ingredient or accompaniment to certain dishes. The sauce is extremely hot and should be used sparingly.

Chinese chicken broth. A basic broth used in Chinese soups and dishes (see recipe on p. 9).

Chinese grater. Small bamboo or ceramic grater with sharp, pointed little teeth used mainly for grating ginger.

Chinese knife. This heavy Chinese cutting knife shaped like a cleaver may look fierce but it is a very useful implement for chopping or for crushing vegetables like leek or ginger with the flat of the blade and scooping up the pieces afterward. The blade can be thick or thin, and is extremely sharp. The thin blades are suitable for boneless meats, vegetables or fruit while the thick ones should be used for meat joints on the bone or for jointing a chicken. The great feature of these knives is the weight and sharpness of the blade, which will always cut clean, leaving in as much of the flavor as possible.

Chinese leaves. Known as *pai t'sai* or *t'sai sum* in China, and *hakusai* or *napa* in Japan, this Chinese cabbage variety with its elongated pale green leaves is now cultivated worldwide and is readily available during the fall and winter months. Commonly used in Eastern cuisine, the leaves can be grated or chopped up in salads or eaten as a hot vegetable in much the same way as Western cabbages which, though different in taste, are perfectly acceptable as substitutes.

Chinese rice. A small, long-grain polished rice which is very low in starch.

Chopsticks. These slender ivory sticks have been in use in China since the Shang Dynasty (1766–1123 B.C.). The first materials included agate, jade, and even silver because it was presumed to blacken on contact with poisoned food. However, ivory, then as now, has always been considered the most suitable.

The ideograms for these utensils have almost the same sound as two others whose transliteration means "male sons" in the West, whence the custom of giving chopsticks as a wedding gift.

Chopsticks are available in two sizes. The shorter size, 10 in long, is used for eating and made of mass market materials like plastic or bamboo as well as lacquered and decorated ivory. The longer, 14-in chopsticks made of bamboo, are for kitchen uses such as beating eggs, mixing sauces or putting individual ingredients in the wok, nimbly executed "to keep the food moving," as the Chinese say.

Chutney (chatni). Widely used sweet and sour Indian pickle made from fruit and spices, usually served with meat in India.

Cinnamon. The perfumed inner bark of the cinnamon tree is one of the most appealing of spices. The easily recognizable small bark sticks are also available in powdered form. *Cinnamomum reylanicum* is an evegreen of the laurel family originating in tropical Asia and grown in many hot countries. An important aromatic ingredient, cinnamon is used in hot spicy curries as well as in puddings, cakes, and pastries.

Clarified butter (ghee). A type of cooking fat which will heat to a high temperature without burning, and is widely used, especially in India (see recipe on p. 9). Ghee can be made from cream instead of butter, and in India it is sometimes flavored with orange or lemon. Authentic ghee is available from specialist grocers and Indian foodshops and should not be confused with varieties made from vegetable substitutes for the vegetarian market.

Coconut. The large fruit of a tropical palm, widely used in Oriental sweet and savory preparations.

Called *kelapa* or *klappa* in Indonesia, and *nariyal* in India, coconut is also a well-known flavoring in Western sweetmeats and can be obtained fresh, dried or canned. Although the brown, fibrous exterior looks fresh the coconut is already drying up by that stage, although the liquid center is still intact. The fresh article has a pale green outer case known as the third layer of protection, which covers the familiar, woody shell or endocarp underneath which is found the white, fleshy lining or seed that encloses the milk.

There are three tests for judging the quality and ripeness of a coconut. The shell should be smooth, without cracks. The milk inside should be audible when the coconut is shaken and the three "eyes" at the base should yield slightly when pressed with the fingers.

The liquid, or milk can be drunk as it is, as can the edible flesh. Both also constitute kitchen ingredients. The flesh is freed from the shell, trimmed and grated or blended in a food processor for making "milk" preparations of different densities, such as the various *santens* in Indonesia. Desiccated coconut is available in powdered form for making cakes or reconstituting as milk for use in the kitchen.

When the coconut has been opened, the flesh will keep for a few days in the refrigerator, covered in water, or it can be grated and deep-frozen.

Coriander. *Coriandrum sativum* is a small umbelliferous plant grown in Europe, North Africa and the East, especially in India, where it is known as *dhnia*. It has light, green heavily-indented leaves and the umbrella-like flowers produce light brown seeds almost the size of peppercorns. Coriander seeds, also available in a powder, are used as a flavoring in Eastern and Western dishes and, with their distinctive aroma, are often included in the preparation of *garam masala* (q.v., see also recipe on p. 10). Fresh coriander leaves are used in salads and chutneys, or as a seasoning and decoration, cut with scissors into little pieces or small sprigs and added before or after cooking, like parsley or chervil.

Cornstarch. Pure cornstarch is light and easily digested. Ingredients are tossed in the flour before cooking, to give the food a pleasing appearance and taste. Cornstarch is also used for thickening sauces or casseroles, diluted in a little water and added at the last minute. Rice flour or potato flour can be used instead.

Cumin. *Cuminum cyminum* and *Cuminum nigrum* are varieties of cumin, an umbelliferous bushy plant originating in Asia and also grown in the Mediterranean basin. The small, fine brownish seeds are highly aromatic, like anise, only more bitter. Cumin is used in many hot and cold dishes and preparations in the East and West. In India, where it is called *zeera* (or *shah zeera* in the darker variety), cumin is one of the essential ingredients of *garam masala* (q.v., see

also p. 10) and is also used in hundreds of other preparations. Cumin is often confused with caraway, which has a similar but stronger taste. Both are used in the liqueur product, Kümmel.

Curry. The English name for Indian *kari*, is generally given to the many inferior versions of this famous Indian sauce that are prepared in the West, from combinations of spices that are not true to Indian culinary customs. Strictly, the term should only apply to the authentic sauce (q.v., see also recipe on p. 10) and to dishes which use the correct curry formula or its permitted variants.

Curry leaves. These leaves (in Latin *Curry patta*) are from a shrub of the citrus family which grows in southern India, Sri Lanka and Pakistan. Available fresh or dried, curry leaves are generally used whole as a flavoring, and are removed and discarded before the dish is served. If they are unobtainable, lemon or orange peel can be used instead.

Curry sauce (kari). A condiment sauce which is characteristic of Indian cuisine in every region (see recipe on p. 10).

Daikon see **Radish, white**.

Deba bocho. A large, very sharp pointed knife, used in Japan for cutting fish and meats.

Fen chiew. A Chinese spirit distilled from sorghum and millet used as a base for *chu yen ching*, a bamboo liqueur.

Fennel seeds. This European umbelliferous with feathery edible leaves has aromatic seeds similar to Indian *mauri* and often confused with aniseed (anise, see **Star anise**), in that they share the same aroma and carminative properties. Fennel can substitute aniseed as a component of Indian five spices (see **Five-spice powder**).

Fenugreek. *Trigonella feonum-graecum*, a spontaneous variety of the pea family, grows profusely in grassy areas all over the world. The aromatic yellow-grey seeds, with their rather bitter caramel taste, are used as a spice. In India, where it is called *methi*, the trefoil leaves are also eaten as a fresh vegetable. Fenugreek is a component of Indian five spice-powder (see **Five-spice powder**).

Fish cake, frozen white. Known as *sazuma age*, this is available from specialist Oriental foodstores.

Fish essence. A strong-smelling condiment from Southeast Asia, known as *nuoc mam* in Kampuchea, Laos and Vietnam, *nam pla* in Thailand and *patis* in the Philippines. The essence or sauce, which is runny and should be used very sparingly, is obtained from the fermentation in jars of fresh, salted anchovies. The first extraction is the best and lightest in color.

Fish flakes, dried. This important Japanese ingredient, known as *katzuobishi*, is indispensable to the preparation of Japanese basic stock and therefore to all dishes that use the stock. The fish, normally bonito, a type of tuna, is first dried then broken into flakes, and is available in this form from Oriental foodshops.

Five-spice powder. An Indian seasoning combining equal amounts of anise, cumin, fenugreek, nigella, and mustard seed. The Chinese version usually includes cinnamon, cloves, pepper, and star anise with or without dried mandarin peel. These and other versions of five spices have a strong, concentrated flavor and modest doses are recommended, whether cooked with the dish or sprinkled on top at the last minute.

Food coloring. Food coloring is an important aspect of Indian gastronomy. Indians love colorful dishes and use saffron and turmeric primarily for that purpose. They have many preparations containing natural or artificial colorants which are used to heighten the appearance of soft drinks, cordials (*sharbats*), sweets or ice creams (*kulfi*) or traditional dishes such as tandoori chicken (*tandoori murghi*). As the vivid, often violent, colors usually have no taste and no food value, they can be omitted when preparing Indian dishes (in some cases, they are perhaps best avoided altogether as they could be a harmful additive). Two important exceptions are saffron and turmeric. These are natural products which make a valid contribution to a dish with their enhancing color and flavor. Genuine saffron (as opposed to substitutes) is very expensive while turmeric is stronger tasting, so Indians tend to use them sparingly, making an infusion with a little hot water which is then stirred into the food, usually rice, already cooked, giving it a particularly pleasant yellowy-orange hue and appetizing flavor.

Galanga. A rhizome similar in appearance and taste to ginger, used mainly in Malaysia and Thailand where it is known respectively as *laos* and *kha*. Small varieties of galanga are ginger-colored while the larger ones are pale-fleshed. It is not as readily available as ginger, which is often used as a substitute. Galanga is available dried or in powdered form. Dried galanga can either be ground or reconstituted in hot water and used like fresh root ginger.

Garam masala. The Indian term, loosely meaning "hot spices," for a prescribed mixture of aromas which are either used on their own or combined with other spices in the preparation of Indian dishes. Readymade *garam masala* powder is easily obtainable from grocers (a homemade version is given on p. 10).

Ghee see **Clarified butter**.

Ginger. *Zingiber officinale* is a tall, herbaceous perennial of the ginger family native to India and Malaysia and grown in tropical areas generally. The fleshy rhizome usually about 4 in long, known gastronomically as root ginger, is used freshly grated, dried or powdered. Sometimes the shoots are dried and used instead. Ginger is of enormous importance in Oriental cuisine, on a par with garlic, onion, and leek. Fresh ginger keeps well in the refrigerator and is available from most vegetable stalls and supermarkets. The delicate balance of sweet fragrance and hot flavor so distinctive of ginger, is partially lost in the dried or powdered product, which tends to be hotter and less aromatic. One of the world's most popular flavorings, ginger is used in cakes and confectionery products, including crystallized ginger. In India, ginger is called *adrak* or *addu* and in Japan, where it is also widely consumed, ginger is known as *shoga*. Thin layers of *shoga* steeped in vinegar, called *gari*, are served with sushi rice. In China, where it is known as *tzian*, ginger is mainly used to counteract stronger flavors. Where ginger juice is called for, grated root ginger is moistened with a drop of water and squeezed through cheesecloth (or commercial ginger juice may be substituted). *Galanga* (q.v.) is similar to ginger and known as *laos* in Malaysia and *kha* in Thailand.

Gingko nuts. A small hard-shelled nut, the gingko is used in many Oriental recipes, both sweet and savory.

Ginseng. A medicinal liquor made from a substance extracted from the root of *panax ginseng*, grown in the Orient for its stimulant properties.

Glutinous rice. An opaque rice common to China with oblong grains which become transparent and sticky when cooked, usually used for puddings and sweet stuffings.

Gomairiki. A small Japanese skillet with a grid-style lid, used for roasting sesame seeds.

Horapa (Thai basil). A wild or cultivated herb peculiar to Thailand, *horapa* is intensely aromatic, with a perfume similar to European basil, especially the very sweet varieties that grow on the Italian riviera which would make an ideal substitute.

Horseradish, green. Known as *wasabi*, this is available in paste or powder form. Its distinctive flavor is used for seasoning raw fish dishes such as *sashimi*.

Hsao mai layers. Dough layers for making steamed Chinese dumplings, or *hsao mai* (see recipe on p. 11).

Huo kuo. A kind of brass chafing-dish about 10 in wide fitted with a small burner and a tube at the center to enable the heat to reach the food. Used chiefly among the Mongolians of northern China, the *huo kuo* is alternatively known as a Mongolian hot pot. Diners sit around the table using chopsticks to dip finely-sliced ingredients (meat, fish or vegetable) into the broth which boils in the *huo kuo* at the center of the table.

Japanese basic stock. There are two kinds: *ichiban dashi* (first stock) and *niban dashi* (second stock). For their preparation *see* p. 9.

Kodai. An Indian skillet.

Kombu *see* **Seaweed**.

Konnyaku. A glutinous substance extracted from Japanese tubers, used to give body to salads and vegetable dishes. Almost tasteless and very low in food value, *konnyaku* is excellent for low-calorie diets. Available loose or in cans.

Krupuk. An Indonesian specialty made of tapioca flour, shrimp or fish and spices, available in packets from Oriental foodshops. A similar Chinese product is available, known as *kapeng*. The flour mixture, cut into strips and rather similar to potato chips in consistency, must be fried in very hot fat until the pieces are swollen and crisp. Kropuk are eaten hot or cold as a cocktail snack, or more likely as a tasty, crunchy garnish for vegetable dishes.

Legumes, dried (pulses). *Dal* is the collective term for the many leguminous products and dishes in India, where pulses form an important part of the national diet. Many varieties are now available in Western supermarkets or health food shops. Among the most typical are the orange-pink lentil *maisur dal*, perhaps the most common of all; *urid dal* or *kolai dal*, white or green-skinned, split soy beans or dark-skinned whole soy; *mug* or *mung dal*, another kind of skinned, split soy bean, usually pale yellow; *chhola dal, chana* or *chenna dal*, varieties of split chick pea, and the small chick pea, *kabil chenna; tuar dal* and *arhar dal*, kinds of yellow, split pea and *lobhia dal*, another pea type; the red bean, *rajma dal*, and so on. All these dried products are pre-pared in the usual way: washed, sorted, and if necessary soaked overnight before cooking, with salt added only at the last minute or after the food is cooked.

Lemon grass. A lemon-scented herb from India, widely cultivated in Sri Lanka and Indonesia where it is known as *sereh*. Lemon grass will also grow indoors in cooler countries, in pots or greenhouses. Heavily scented when fresh, the long blue-green stems proceed from a bulbous base, which is the best end to use when slicing in food. It is also available chopped and dried, or in powdered form. The dried product needs soaking before use. In the absence of lemon grass, grated lemon peel will make an acceptable substitute.

Lentil flour. A flour extracted from the Indian lentil, *maisur dal*, used mainly for making a type of flat biscuit, served plain or buttered as snacks or as a garnish or accompaniment to certain dishes, rather like poppadums (q.v.). Lentil biscuits are available in packets from specialist shops.

Lotus root. Used mainly in China in soups and vegetable dishes, lotus root is mildly sweet with a crunchy texture, very hard to find fresh. It is sold in dried slices or in cans. Crystallized lotus root, a sweet delicacy, is also available.

Mace. Known in India as *jaitri*, mace is the fleshy outer covering of the nutmeg (q.v.). Red when fresh, mace turns yellow when dried and develops a stronger taste than the nutmeg it encloses. Mace is sold as a powder or in desiccated strips and should be used sparingly.

Mandarin pancakes. Very thin little pancakes (see recipe on p. 9) served mainly as an accompaniment to Peking duck.

Mango. A fruit-bearing Malaysian evergreen widely propagated in tropical countries. The fragrant fruit, resembling a large peach, has a sweet, pleasant-tasting flesh. In India ripe mango, known as *amra o am*, is either eaten fresh or made into cookies. Underripe mango is used in certain meat and vegetable dishes, or for making drinks and chutneys, *am achar* or *am chatni*. As a flavoring, mango is milder than tamarind (q.v.), though in function the two are similar. Tamarind flesh is dried then reconstituted and squeezed for its juice while mango is dried and pounded to a powder. This powder, known as *sam choor*, is a convenient substitute for tamarind when the latter is unavailable.

Mao tai. A sorghum-based Chinese liquor with an alcoholic content of 55°.

Melon pulp, dried. Available from specialist foodstores, this is used in some Oriental dishes.

Milk concentrate. *Khoya* or *khoa* are the Indian names for a homemade type of evaporated milk used for cooking which tastes quite different from the canned versions. Rich milk is brought to boiling point and reduced over slow heat for 1–1$\frac{1}{2}$ hours depending on how thin, creamy or solid the end product should be. The solidifying action turns the milk a deep yellow-orange.

Mirin. This sweet Japanese rice wine is used as a dressing or for cooking. It is available from Oriental foodshops and rather expensive. Sweet sherry, sweet white vermouth or, more successfully, saké with a little sugar added will serve as substitutes.

Miso see **Soy**.

Momiyashi see **Soy**.

Monosodium glutamate. A chemical product extracted from seaweeds and other vegetable matter, used extensively in Oriental cuisine and elsewhere as a flavoring, especially in packaged food products. There are many brand names for monosodium glutamate, often referred to in the United States as MSG, in Japan as *aji no moto* and in China as *ve tain*. Although the small white crystals should be used very sparingly, there are some more or less justifiable doubts in certain quarters regarding the possible harmful effects of monosodium glutamate. The product is included in the recipes of this book for the sake of authenticity but its use is not strictly necessary.

Mung beans see **Soy**.

Mug dal flour. An Indian flour obtained from *mug dal* or *mung dal*, a type of soy bean. The bean is first roasted, then ground to produce the flour. This type of flour, known in India as

chatu, is edible as it is, mixed with sugar, or it can be made into baps or pancakes. If the bean is ground only, it produces a flour type known as *beshon* or *besan* which can also be used for making cakes and puddings.

Mushrooms, dried. Oriental mushrooms are generally tougher in texture than European mushrooms and are very different in taste and smell. A common feature in Eastern preparations, dried mushrooms are available in the West and must be soaked in warm water before use. The flavored soaking water is usually strained and subsequently added to the ingredients during cooking. Well-known varieties are the Japanese *shiitake* and particularly the Chinese *tung-ku*, considered to have the best flavor. Only the cap is eaten, the stalk being far too tough. Chinese food shops also stock less scented types such as the fungus or cup mushroom. Mushrooms are also widely used in Thailand and Vietnam.

Nabé. A covered terracotta casserole used in Japan for cooking at table. It must be dried thoroughly before being exposed to heat.

Nam pla see **Fish essence**.

Nigella. A herbaceous plant grown widely in the Mediterranean and in its variety, *Nigella sativa*, also cultivated in Oriental countries, notably India, where it is named *kalajira*. The spicy, dark triangular seeds have been used for centuries as a seasoning and in India, nigella has also since ancient times been taken

medicinally. It is one of spices included in Indian five-spice powder (see **Five-spice powder**).

Noodles (mung bean, transparent, cellophane). Also made in thin strips, these thread-like transparent noodles are normally soaked in water for ten minutes before cooking. They are commonly used in Asian preparations.

Noodles (rice). A fine noodle made from rice flour, also typically Asian. Available from specialist shops.

Nori see **Seaweed**.

Nuoc mam see **Fish essence**.

Nutmeg. The hard fruit of the nutmeg tree (*Myristica fragrans*), an evergreen native to Malaysia and the Moluccan Islands, grown widely in Indonesia and other hot countries, particularly India. Its fleshy casing constitutes the dried product known as mace (q.v.). The fragrant, brown kernel, *pala* in Indonesia, *jatiphala* or *jayphala* in India, is also widely used in the West, freshly grated or ground.

Onion grains. The seeds from the flower of this Indian onion variety, known as *kalongi*, are used in salad dishes and desserts.

Oyster sauce. *Hou you*, as it is known in China, is a condiment sauce, used as a flavoring in various preparations. Available in small pots or bottles, the sauce, which is brown and rather thick, is obtained by reducing a mixture of oyster juice

and salted soy sauce.

Panir. An Indian home-made curd cheese.

Peanut oil. Also known as groundnut oil, this is a versatile, fragrant oil much used in Oriental cuisine.

Peanut sauce (sans katjang). An Indonesian salad dressing used also as a side dish to accompany various Eastern preparations (see recipe on p. 10).

Pepper. Arguably the most widely used spice in the world, pepper derives from *Piper nigrum*, a spontaneous climbing plant with twining branches, probably originating in Indonesia and cultivated throughout tropical Asia and equatorial America. The green berries turn red when ripe (and are sometimes pickled in this form), after which they are dried in the sun, either whole or skinned (white pepper). Pepper has different names in the Orient, and should not be confused with the lesser-known Jamaican pimento, fruit of a local variety *Pimenta officinalis*. Pepper is one of the spices included in the preparation of *garam masala* (q.v., see also recipe on p. 10). For its full effect, pepper should be used freshly milled as required.

Poppadums or pappa-dums. A type of Oriental griddle bread, most common to India, particularly in the northern regions where they are known as *paaper*. Poppadums are usually spiced or plain. They are almost impossible to make at home, partly because in some areas the right kinds of flour (lentil or chick pea) are hard to find and partly because their preparation, which requires rolling flour paste into razor-thin circles of up to 12 in in diameter, is almost too daunting to contemplate. Temperature and other conditions have to be right, too. Poppadums are highly absorbent and will deteriorate quickly if exposed to damp. This added obstacle is also why, in India, they are only made during the dry season.

Poppadums are available in sealed packs ready for use from most supermarkets. Once the pack is opened, the poppadums should be cooked and served immediately, as a snack or a crisp bread, either accompanying a dish or crumbled over it. Spicy poppadums are delicious on their own or served with mild dishes, while the plain ones usually accompany hot dishes. They are cooked in various ways.

When deep-frying, allow for the dough to expand by using a larger saucepan than seemingly necessary, or by cutting the dough into smaller portions. Care should be taken to dust off any specks of flour or other matter which might contaminate the oil. For successful results, the heat of the oil must remain constant. The cooking process requires a little skill. Poppadums turn color immediately and should be cooked no more than a couple of seconds on either side then swiftly removed from the oil to dry on kitchen towels and eaten at once. It is essential to remove poppadums from the heat in time otherwise they will burn and appear unsightly.

If the broiling method is preferred, the broiler must be preheated, with the heat at a minimum height of 2 in above the food. The poppadums will expand under the heat and must be turned and removed as soon as bubbling occurs, to avoid burning.

Poppadums can also be cooked over a direct source of heat, held gently between the fingers and slowly rotated until evenly crisped. This method, however, is not recommended for the novice or inexperienced cooks.

Poppy seed. The minute white seeds of the poppy have various uses, one of them being the extraction of oil. In India, where this is called *khaskhas*, it is used widely in certain preparations and also as a thickener.

Radish, white. Known as *Daikon* by the Japanese, this carrot-shaped alternative to the Western radish is sold fresh in good-quality supermarkets. White radish is extremely hot.

Rice flour. Rice flour, finely ground white or brown rice, is widely used in Oriental cuisine. It is used to make the dough for rice flour noodles.

Rice wine. This Japanese fermented liquor, known internationally as *saké*, is also manufactured in other Oriental countries, notably China. It has an alcoholic content of about 17°. As well as being a meal time drink, saké is used in the kitchen as a sauce flavoring. A sweet version called *mirin* (q.v.) is manufactured for cooking purposes. In most cases, dry sherry will adequately substitute *saké*.

Rice wine vinegar or rice vinegar. A vinegar made from fermented rice wine. There are Chinese and Japanese versions, ranging in flavor from mild to sharp.

Rose water. A perfumed essence extracted from rose petals known since ancient times in the East and West and still produced in quantity in some Eastern countries as a food flavoring. Rose water is available from chemists and Oriental food shops. Also available is a concentrated version which must be used very sparingly, one drop at a time.

Saffron. Pure saffron is obtained from the orange-colored stigmas of the violet crocus *Crocus sativus*, a perennial originating in the Middle East and grown in many areas. The product itself, however, is chiefly associated with Oriental countries, notably India, where it is known as *zafran* or *kesar*. The commercial powdered versions usually contain a larger element of turmeric and coriander than genuine saffron. This is because saffron is by nature scarce and expensive to produce. It is estimated that 100,000 flowers are needed to obtain 2 lb of stigma threads, or $2^{1}/_{2}$ acres of land for a yield of 20–30 lb. These costly, tiny threads are available whole from specialist grocers and Oriental shops. Only a very small amount is needed to gain a desirable color and aroma. The threads are first ground in a mortar, or placed in a small bag and crushed with a mallet; then diluted in a little broth, water or milk, depending on the recipe.

Sago (or sagú). A starchy substance obtained from the pith of different palms in tropical countries.
Saké see **Rice wine**.

Sambal see **Chili pepper**.

Santen see **Coconut**.

Sea cucumber. The sea slug (or cucumber) found in Indian and Pacific waters is a popular delicacy in Oriental countries, particularly China, where it is known as *trepang*. The off-putting appearance is compensated by a rather pleasant taste. In dried form, sea cucumber will keep indefinitely and should be soaked in water for at least 3 days before use.

Seaweed. In Oriental countries, seaweed is commonly used as a food. Many preparations include seaweed in China and particularly in Japan, where it is believed to be exceptionally nutritious and invigorating. The Japanese prepare seaweed for the commercial market dried and packaged in layers or other convenient forms which will keep almost indefinitely. It is worth identifying the main varieties used in the preparation of traditional Japanese dishes, and normally available from Oriental foodstores.

Kombu is an essential ingredient of Japanese basic stock (*dashi*). It is prepared in dried strips which give it a bark-like, almost black appearance. When the strips have been rinsed and softened in hot water, they are ready to use: seaweed must never be boiled. The powdered version of *kombu*, sold in cans, is

161

used for making *kombusha*, a hot tonic drink, also called seaweed tea, which is more of a pick-me-up than a regular food.

Nori is perhaps the best known and widely used of the edible seaweeds. Many will be familiar with the purplish-black wrappers for rice rolls; *nori* is also an important flavoring for omelets and soups. It is available in layers, small blocks or strips (also chopped or crumbled). These should be prepared and used preferably with food that is already cooked, or added to the saucepan at the last minute. Being highly scented and fragile in texture, *nori* would also be spoiled in soups unless it was added at the last minute.

Wakame, also a dried product, is used in soups and, combined with other ingredients, in salads. Contact with water will transform *wakame* from a blackish skein into slippery green leaves which should be rinsed before use.

Tororo, another seaweed normally used in soups (with or in lieu of *nori*). Silky gold in appearance, with a mushroom-like scent, it is used to give body and flavor to the soup.

Finally *hijiki*, the only true vegetable among them, is dark and dried like the rest and must be softened in warm water for about 30 minutes before cooking.

Sesame seed oil. This highly aromatic seed oil is used in dressings, sauces, pickling, and preserves. It should be added very sparingly. Sesame seed oil is unsuitable for frying because the aroma is so pronounced. To preserve this essential feature, the oil is sold in small bottles for quick consumption. Available in supermarkets, sesame seed oil is virtually irreplaceable as an ingredient. Called *goma abura* in Japan and *zima you* in China, it is widely used in Oriental countries.

Sesame paste. A condiment made from pressing white sesame seeds, sold in glass containers to preserve the strong sesame scent and taste. The paste, which is rather dense, is usually diluted in stock or soy sauce mixed with vinegar and used as a dressing for braised pork dishes.

Sesame sauce (goma zu). A highly-flavored sesame product from Japan (*see* recipe on p. 10).

Sesame seeds. The seeds of a type of bushy plant originating in Africa and India and cultivated throughout Asia, especially in China, India, and Japan. The plant has pink or white flowers which sprout long pods full of seed. These seeds are either black or white, depending on the species, and are crushed to make sesame seed oil (q.v.).

Sesame seeds are used in many preparations, bread and pastry products and spice compounds such as five-spice powder (q.v.). The whole grains, with their well known, nutty aroma taste even better when they have been cooked or roasted.

In Japan, sesame seeds, or *goma*, are toasted with salt to make a condiment known as *goma shio*. In India, where the seeds are named *til*, sesame is also used as a substitute for almonds. The Chinese mainly use the white seeds, or *zi ma*, for preparing sesame paste (q.v.) and dishes that incorporate it, and for garnishing sweetmeats and flavoring stuffings, while the black seeds have a similar function in a traditional Chinese version of trifle.

Shao shing. A Chinese liqueur made from a blend of glutinous rice, plain rice and millet, with an alcohol content not exceeding 19°. Shao shing is usually aged for ten years before it goes on sale. The finest-quality shao shing is more than 50 years old.

Sharbat. This is the collective name for the dozens of brightly colored, different flavored syrup drinks that are a common and vivid sight on Indian streets, where vendors sell the *sharbats* with ice topped with water and in certain cases, additional sugar.

Shark's fin. *Yui tzi* in Chinese, shark's fin is available dried and prepackaged from Chinese food shops. It is used to prepare the soup that bears its name.

Shiitake. A Japanese dried mushroom similar to the noted Chinese variety. *Shiitake* must be soaked in warm water for at least 1 hour before cooking (*see* **Mushrooms, dried**).

Shirataki. Meaning literally "white cascade," *shirataki* is a type of Japanese noodle made from *konnyaku* (q.v.).

Shrimp paste. A concentrated canned product used mainly in Indonesian dishes, made from shrimp ground to a paste. Unlike some similar-named Western products, this paste has a strong taste and, used sparingly, provides a delicious flavoring. The product is available from specialist shops under different names, depending on the country of origin: *Ngapi* from Burma, *kapi* from Thailand, *blachan* from Malaysia, and *trasi* from Indonesia.

Shrimp, dried. These may be used dried, or soaked in water before use, and are widely used in Oriental cuisine, notably in Chinese or Southeast Asian recipes.

Silver leaf. Renaissance documents show that gold and silver have long been in use as an edible garnish. In India edible silver leaf, known as *waraq*, is used to decorate elegant dishes and festive meals, pastries or *paans* (*see* **Betel**). Indians and Indonesians, consider that *waraq* has tonic properties and helps the digestion.

Soy. A herbaceous plant originating in China and Japan, soy is now cultivated worldwide. Its fruit, the soy bean, plays a very important part in the Oriental diet. There are countless products deriving from soy. Soy bean curd (q.v.), also known as tofu, is one of the most popular. Another soy product, bean sprouts, known as *momiyashi* in Japan and *ya tsai* in China, is widely available in the West. These slender, pale little sprouts, usually eaten fresh or blanched, derive from the green soy bean, or *mung* bean, which is also the source of the fine, transparent soy bean noodle (see **Noodles, mung bean**). Another type of soy bean, particularly common in Japan, is the red *aduki* bean. The white soy bean also has many uses.

A classic soy product is the Japanese preparation, *miso*, obtained by reducing the bean to a paste then fermenting it. The main varieties, *aka miso* (red) and *shiro miso* (white), are used chiefly as thickeners or as a base for sauces. Versions of *miso* are made in China and other Oriental countries. Probably the best known internationally of these Oriental soy products is soy sauce (or soya sauce), readily available in the West and omnipresent in Oriental cuisine as a condiment or flavoring. There are two types – light and dark. A Chinese alternative, *hoisin* sauce, sweeter and lighter in flavor, with added sugar, spices, thickener and red food coloring, is often used in the West as barbecue sauce.

Soy bean curd (tofu). Cooked, pulped, and specially treated soy beans behave in the same way as animal milk, in that they react to acid coagulants by curdling. The substance produced is like fresh, almost tasteless cheese; easily digestible and rich in protein, it is widely used in Oriental cooking or as a vegetarian food.

In Japan, *tofu* is prepared for the market in cubes, layers or freeze-dried. It is available in 10-oz cakes from health food shops and Oriental restaurants or stores and will keep for a few days immersed in water in the refrigerator. However, the handiest and most frequently used *tofu* is in small blocks which can be easily cut up ready for cooking.

Soy paste See **Soy**.

Soy sauce see **Soy**.

Star anise. A plant of the magnolia family, the star anise, *Illicium anisatum*, is native to China and grown throughout the Far East. The name derives from the 8–12 radially displayed follicles containing oval licorice-flavored seeds widely used in Oriental pastries and sauces. Star anise, known in China as *pa-co-hu-huai-hiam* and in India as *sauf*, is the Oriental counterpart of green anise, *Pimpinella anisum*, a widespread herb grown also in Europe, with seeds known as aniseed. Though similar, star anise should not be confused with the sweeter-tasting aniseed, a popular flavoring for liquors and confectionery. Fennel seed should also not be mistaken for aniseed or its parent name green anise, as sometimes happens.

Sudare. A flexible table mat made of bamboo, used in Japan for preparing rice rolls or vegetable rolls.

Suribachi. An earthenware bowl of Japanese origin with grooves on the inside, used for mincing or crushing ingredients with a mallet.

Tamago. A Japanese rectangular omelet skillet with a long handle.

Tamarind. The pod-like fruit of the tropical tamarind is virtually unobtainable fresh in Western countries. In India, where it is known as *imli*, and in other parts of Southeast Asia, its bitter juice is used to accentuate flavors and freshen sauces. Tamarind is also the basis of a drink called *imli ka pani*. Dried tamarind blocks are available for making tamarind water. A piece from the block is soaked in warm water for about $1/2$ hour, then squeezed, adding the juice to the water. The process can be repeated if necessary. Concentrated tamarind water is also available.

Tapioca. A starchy white-grained substance which is obtained from the cassava plant and used in puddings.

Taro. The Chinese name for this tropical root vegetable is *wo tou*, sticky potato. Similar to the potato, it has rough, dark skin and hard, white flesh with red traces and glutinous fibers in it. The taste is more delicate than the common potato though this would be a perfectly adequate substitute.

Tava. An iron plate used in India for cooking chapatis and other griddle breads.

Tea. Tea is one of seven cardinal ingredients which, according to an old Chinese proverb, the housewife must never be without (the others being fire, rice, oil, salt, soy sauce, and vinegar). The custom of tea-drinking is deeply rooted in Chinese culture and has its own set of rules. Tea is served before and after, only rarely during a meal. It celebrates every daytime occasion, however, trivial, and it is the standard welcome drink wherever hospitality is being offered. Out of hundreds of varie-ties of Chinese tea, there are six main types: green tea (unfermented), black tea (fermented), oolong (semi-fermented), white tea (very delicate), scented tea (flower-blended), and infusions. *Pu erh*, is a black tea of high quality, good for the digestion and low in cholestorol while the scented jasmine variety is probably the most widely known outside China.

The custom in Japan is to serve tea with pickles, always at the end of a meal. Tea is of great importance in Japan, and there are four main types. *Matcha*, a powdered green variety, used in the tea ceremony; *bancha*, a toasted tea for everyday use; *gyokuro*, a superior, strongly scented green tea and *shincha*, a green, leaf variety, the one used at the end of meals with the rice and pickles (for the preparation of tea, see p. 12).

Thandai. A very popular Indian spiced milk drink also known as *kes-her-doodh* (see recipe on p. 12).

Tofu see **Soy bean curd**.

Turmeric. There are some 50 species of turmeric, a large-leaved plant with brilliant spiky flowers, native to Southeast Asia and Australia. Some species have an aromatic rhizome of which the flesh, white or yellow, is dried then ground to a flour constituting the yellow dye (curcumin, or turmeric) which, combined with certain alkali, takes on a reddish hue.

Similar in color effect to saffron, turmeric otherwise bears no comparison to the former and its use as a substitute in saffron dishes should be avoided if authenticity is the keynote. The floury powder has specific properties that extend beyond the kitchen. Turmeric is a useful diuretic and bowel regulator and in some parts of India, where it is known as *haldi* or *holud*, it is applied as a cosmetic and disinfectant. However, like saffron, it is used mostly in food as a colorant and flavoring.

Udon. Large wheat noodles of Japan which are boiled and rinsed in cold water prior to cooking.

Usuba bocho. A heavy, very sharp Japanese knife shaped like a cleaver, used for cutting vegetables.

Wakame see **Seaweed**.

Wasabi see **Horseradish, green**.

Wok. The traditional cast-iron *wok* is a centuries-old frying utensil known in China as *kuo*. The curved base is ideal for distributing the heat and the condiments evenly around the food. Woks come in various sizes, either with two iron handles or one wooden handle.

A new iron wok needs to be seasoned before it is used for the first time. First it is washed, rinsed thoroughly and dried with kitchen towels. Then peanut oil is smeared all over the inside and cooked for 5 or 6 minutes over high heat. The wok is removed from the heat and, with great care, rinsed immediately under hot water and dried once more with kitchen towels. Repeat this operation, cooking the oil for 1 minute instead of 5, until the kitchen towels

wipe off clean.

After use, the wok should be washed in plain hot water and dried for a second or two over the heat. Liquid detergents should never be used.

Special iron rests are available from specialist shops, for holding the wok steady on modern hobs.

A wok for domestic use should be 12–14 in in diameter. Anything smaller would make stir-frying difficult, even if there are only a few ingredients to cook. If too large, the heat would be too diffused to cook the food efficiently.

Wonton wrappers. A paper-thin Chinese pastry used to fold around a meat and vegtetable filling before being fried (see recipe on p. 9).

Wu chia pi. A Chinese liquor prepared from sorghum and caramelized barley sugar, which gives it its slightly burnt taste, similar to madeira. *Wu chia pi* is said to be good for the blood circulation and an excellent digestive aid. It is used in preparation of certain gourmet meat dishes.

Zaru. A shallow round Oriental sifter made of bamboo.

Index